Serlene Varieties
P/61
92-102

TEACHING ENGLISH GRAMMAR

Teaching
English Grammar

ROBERT C. POOLEY

University of Wisconsin

New York

APPLETON-CENTURY-CROFTS, INC.

To

E. A. CROSS

grammarian, teacher, friend

this book is gratefully dedicated

Preface

IN THE CURRENT SETTING of grammar teaching in the United States it is perhaps more foolhardy than courageous to offer a book on the subject. On the one hand the forces of tradition and conservatism cling so firmly to grammar as a school subject that anyone who ventures to suggest changes in content and method is condemned in advance. In direct contrast, the experimental endeavors of contemporary linguists have laid so bare the inadequacies of traditional grammar as the means to the study of English that anyone fairly familiar with their work hesitates to refer to the older terminology of grammar, much less to advocate its use. Yet somehow this chasm must be bridged. English grammar has a useful part to play in the training of young people to use their language effectively. Those who teach grammar need help in determining exactly what is meant by the term, what content it does and does not include, for what purposes it is properly to be used, and what outcomes may be expected from its use.

Many and serious confusions exist regarding the nature, use, and outcomes of grammar instruction. To clarify some of these confusions, to distinguish the particular contribution which grammar may make to the education of young people, and to present a workable, reasonable plan to accomplish these educational goals is the purpose of this book. No one is more aware of its many shortcomings than the author. Although many difficulties are involved, he finds courage in the hope that despite almost irreconcilable conflicts of idea and opinion among current practitioners of English grammar, this book may offer a compromise position and plan for those who wish to teach grammar, and may in time assist the union of tradition and experimentation which seems to be the manifest destiny of English grammar.

In the preparation of this book many scholars and teachers have indirectly contributed by their lectures, conversations, and writings. Thanks to all such in general is expressed here, and in particular by footnote reference throughout the book. In the composition of the manuscript the writer is deeply indebted to the research aid rendered by Mrs. Doris Vinocur and Miss Marion Metcalf. While the author accepts full responsibility for any errors of fact or implication which may be found, he has been spared the embarrassment of many more by the careful reading of manuscript and proof-sheets by Professors John R. Searles of the University of Wisconsin, and Fred G. Walcott of the University of Michigan, to whom he gives grateful thanks. Further thanks go to Mrs. Margaret Hundt for the carefully corrected typescript.

R. C. P.

Contents

ix

TEACHING ENGLISH GRAMMAR

I

What Is Grammar?

NEARLY EVERY TEACHER OF ENGLISH who owns to his profession publicly has learned to expect some such reaction as this: "So you're an English teacher!" An awkward pause usually follows, and then comes the almost inevitable remark, "I never did like grammar!" The average ex-student, recalling hours spent in memorizing rules in a vain attempt to bring his speech and writing into conformity with some inflexible pedagogical ideal of "pure" and "correct" English, is apt to regard many English teachers with distaste if not dislike.

Just what is this grammar, so often of unpleasant memory? What does the term mean now, and what has it meant in the past? An examination of the sources of the word itself may help us to answer these questions.

DERIVATION OF *GRAMMAR*

The ultimate root of the English word *grammar* is the Greek word *graphein*, to write. From the root of *graphein* comes the word *gramma*, letter, written mark, and from the plural of *gramma*, *grammata*, comes the adjective *grammatikos*, of or pertaining to letters or literature, the feminine of which, *grammatike*, becomes in Latin *grammatica*. The Old French *gramaire*, an irregular adoption from the Latin form, becomes the Middle English *gram(m)ere*, from which Modern English *grammar* is derived.

The *New English Dictionary* tells us that in classical Greek and Latin the word *grammar* denoted "the methodical study of

1

literature . . . including textual and aesthetic criticism, investigation of literary history and antiquities, explanation of allusions,
etc., besides the study of the Greek and Latin languages." As its
sources themselves clearly indicate, the term was indeed equal to
the term "*philology* in the widest modern sense."

In the Middle Ages grammar was the first subject of the *trivium*,
which included also logic and rhetoric. Grammar, for medieval
man, meant the study of the Latin language and Latin literature.

The Latin language contained the sum of knowledge transmitted to
the Middle Ages. And it had to be learned. . . . Centuries before the
Roman youth had studied grammar that they might speak and write
correctly. Now it was necessary to study Latin grammar, to wit, the
true forms and literary usages of the Latin tongue, in order to acquire
any branch of knowledge whatsoever, and express one's corresponding
thoughts. [1]

Here, too, the *grammar* included in its meaning what we should
consider literature. This fact is born out by John of Salisbury's
description of the teaching method followed by Bernard of
Chartres:

By citations from the authors he showed what was simple and regular; he brought into relief the grammatical figures, the rhetorical
colours, the artifices of sophistry, and pointed out how the text in hand
bore upon other studies. . . . He inculcated correctness and propriety
of diction, and a fitting use of congruous figures. Realizing that
practice strengthens memory and sharpens faculty, he urged his pupils
to imitate what they had heard, inciting some by admonitions, others
by whipping and penalties. Each pupil recited the next day something
from what he had heard on the preceding. The evening exercise, called
the *declinatio*, was filled with such an abundance of grammar that
anyone, of fair intelligence, by attending it for a year, would have at
his finger's ends the art of writing and speaking and would know the
meaning of all words in common use. [2]

Bernard, then, made much use of literature in his teaching of
grammar, and this appears to have been the custom generally.

---

[1] Henry Osborn Taylor, *The Mediaeval Mind* (London, Macmillan & Co.,
Ltd., 1938), Vol. II, p. 361.
[2] *Ibid.*, p. 157.

The term *grammar*, meaning knowledge of Latin language and literature, knowledge peculiar to the learned class, was sometimes used, says the *N.E.D.*, as synonymous with learning in general in the Middle Ages. It is interesting to note that we owe our word *glamour* to the idea that magic and astrology were part of the "learning in general" to which the O.F. *gramaire* was applied. Some students may be unwilling to admit even an etymological connection between *glamour* and *grammar!*

GRAMMAR TRANSFERRED TO ENGLISH

Until the seventeenth century the term *grammar* in English usage meant the study of Latin—hence a "grammar school" was originally one in which Latin was taught. Very little work was done in English grammar. Ben Jonson's *English Grammar*, written *c.* 1600 and published in 1640, was one of the first books, according to the *N.E.D.*, to deal with the subject under its own name. Jonson's grammar shows everywhere the influence of his study of Latin and Greek, despite the claim made in the title that it was "made by Ben Jonson, for the benefit of all strangers, out of his observation of the English language, now spoken and in use." [3]

The rise of the middle class in the eighteenth century brought about a great demand for grammars. People with new leisure for the pursuit of culture demanded rules for "correctness" in language, and rules were provided in great plenty. Most of the grammarians of the eighteenth century followed the precedent set by Ben Jonson and others in the seventeenth century—they modeled their grammars of English on the Latin grammars. Most of them divided the study of grammar into four or five parts: Orthography, Etymology, Syntax, Prosody, and sometimes Orthoëpy. [4] Teaching grammar meant to them teaching students to write and to speak according to the rules. The fact that the rules were often arbitrary or based on personal prejudice seemed not at

[3] For detailed evidence of Jonson's dependence on Latin in this work, see Roland G. Kent, *Language and Philology* (Boston, Marshall Jones Co., 1923), pp. 134–137.
[4] *N.E.D.*

all to disturb those who expounded them. They did not hesitate to point out "errors" in the works of England's greatest authors. This attitude Fries called "the doctrine of original sin" in grammar. [5]

THE PRESCRIPTIVE NOTION OF GRAMMAR

The eighteenth-century philosophy of prescriptive grammar was carried over into most of the grammars produced in the nineteenth century and even into our own times. In the nineteenth century, however, we find the beginnings of a new concept—descriptive grammar, based on scientific studies of the history of languages and of usage. The Romantic Movement, with its interest in the exotic and ancient, brought in its train the frame of mind necessary to appreciate the rediscovery of Sanskrit, and hence the beginnings of really scientific language studies. [6] The work of R. K. Rask, J. L. C. Grimm, A. F. Pott, A. Frick, and others made clear some of the relationships among languages and the nature of the changes which occur in them. F. Max Müller's *Lectures on the Science of Language*, published at Oxford in 1861 and 1864, helped to make the results of this work known in England. [7] For those who applied the results of these studies to English, grammar came to mean observation and description of the language as it is spoken and written, and an attempt to determine how it came to assume its present form. By 1910 we find A. H. Sayce writing an article on grammar for the 11th edition of the *Encyclopaedia Britannica* in which he says flatly:

Grammatical propriety is nothing more than the established usage of a particular body of speakers at a particular time in their history. . . . The idea that the free use of speech is tied down by the rules of the grammarians . . . must be given up; all that the grammarian can do is

[5] Charles C. Fries, *The Teaching of the English Language* (New York, Thomas Nelson and Sons, 1927), p. 17.

[6] Leonard Bloomfield, *Introduction to the Study of Language* (New York, Henry Holt and Co., 1914), p. 309.

[7] For a discussion of the development of language studies, see Louis H. Gray, *Foundations of Language* (New York, The Macmillan Co., 1939), pp. 419–460.

to formulate the current uses of his time, which are determined by habit and custom, and are accordingly in a perpetual state of flux. *We must get rid of the notion that English grammar should be modeled after that of ancient Rome;* until we do, we shall never understand even the elementary principles upon which it is based. [Italics mine.]

Expressions of very similar attitudes toward grammar can be found in the works of such distinguished students of language as Otto Jespersen, Leonard Bloomfield, and George P. Krapp.

The fact that many people still cling to the eighteenth-century notion of grammar is in large part due to resistance to change on the part of schools and school teachers. It is to be hoped that in the future increasing numbers of English teachers will be convinced of the truth of Jespersen's statement that "the essence of language is human activity," and that like human activity, it is subject to change; that words and forms are not "things or natural objects with an existence of their own," but tools which may be modified by those who use them. [8]

In this book the word *grammar* will refer to the structure of English, the way English works when it is used for the communication of ideas. Further definitions will be found in Chapter IX.

REFERENCES

BLOOMFIELD, Leonard, *Introduction to the Study of Language* (New York, Henry Holt and Co., 1914).

FRIES, Charles C., *The Teaching of the English Language* (New York, Thomas Nelson and Sons, 1927).

JESPERSEN, Otto, *The Philosophy of Grammar* (New York, Henry Holt and Co., 1924).

KENT, Roland G., *Language and Philology* (Boston, Marshall Jones Co., 1923).

LEONARD, Sterling Andrus, *The Doctrine of Correctness in English Usage, 1700–1800,* University of Wisconsin Studies in Language and Literature, No. 25 (Madison, Wis., 1929), p. 192.

TAYLOR, Henry Osborn, *The Mediaeval Mind* (London, Macmillan & Co., Ltd., 1938).

[8] Otto Jespersen, *The Philosophy of Grammar* (New York, Henry Holt and Co., 1924), p. 2.

II
The Development of Grammar

FROM VERY EARLY PERIODS, man has been concerned with solving the riddle of the origin of languages. The story of the Tower of Babel in the book of Genesis represents one attempt to account for the diversity of tongues; the explanation given there, it will be remembered, is that when men in their pride attempted to build a tower reaching to the heavens, God caused confusion of tongues, thus forcing them to abandon their project. The many attempts at etymology in the Old Testament also show an early interest in the history and meanings of words. An example of such popular or folk etymologies is the Biblical explanation that the term *Babel* (Babylon) was given to the place where the ill-fated tower was begun "because the Lord did there confound the language of all the earth."[1]

Real language study begins, however, with what Gray calls "the two great thinking peoples of antiquity," those of India and those of Greece.[2] Of the Indian grammarians, whose interest in grammar was primarily analytical, the greatest was Panini, who wrote an authoritative grammar of Sanskrit at the end of the fourth century B.C. This is the first formal grammar of which we have any knowledge, and it "consists of some four thousand very brief statements of linguistic phenomena, most of them designated by arbitrary sounds or complexes of sounds used as code-words."[3] The Indian

[1] Louis H. Gray, *Foundations of Language* (New York, The Macmillan Co., 1939), p. 419.
[2] *Ibid.*, p. 421.

6

grammars were primarily designed to enable people to read traditional esthetic and religious works. [4]

PHILOSOPHIES OF GRAMMAR

In Greece, speculation about language assumed a more philosophical character. The earliest example which we possess of the Greek attempts to study language is the *Crotylus* of Plato, which gives some rather inaccurate etymologies and sets forth the idea, apparently held earlier by Pythagoras and Heraclitus, that language has arisen "by nature"—that is, out of some inherent necessity. In general, the Stoic philosophers agreed with Plato in this notion about the origin of language. Here, however, as in so many other areas of knowledge, Aristotle is the first really important figure. He "may be regarded as the father of grammar in the Occidental World." He began the study of the parts of speech, cases, and gender. As to the origin of language, he agreed, not with Plato and his predecessors, but with Democritus, that language is the result of "convention" or "agreement," an opinion in which the Epicureans generally concurred. [5]

As the study of language in Greece developed, another controversy arose to complicate further that already created by the difference of opinion between the Platonists and the Aristotelians about the origin of language. This was the controversy between the Analogists and the Anomalists. The point of view of the Anomalists, of whom the most important was Crates of Mallos, was very close to that of modern students of language: they held that grammatical rules are established by custom and are therefore subject to change. The Analogists, on the contrary, stated that there is a strict law of analogy between the idea and the word, and insisted upon absolute, unchanging grammatical rules. The Analo-

---

3 *Ibid.*

4 Leonard Bloomfield, *Introduction to the Study of Language* (New York, Henry Holt and Co., 1914), p. 307.

5 Gray, *op. cit.*, p. 423.

gists eventually triumphed, and Dionysius Thrax, pupil of the Analogist Aristarchus, wrote a Greek grammar in the first century B.C. which became a model for most Latin grammars in Rome. Donatus, in the fourth century A.D., and Priscian, about 500 A.D., wrote grammars after the pattern set by Dionysius; and these two grammars, in turn, set the pattern for most of the Latin and Greek grammars written in the Middle Ages and for the vernacular grammars which followed:

The grammatical apparatus developed and available in the sixteenth century when the first practical grammars of the vernacular arose was this which had been used for centuries for the Latin language—it is the dead hand of the old Analogist group of the second century B.C. [6]

As Gray points out, Christianity influenced all things, including the study of language. The early Church Fathers, Saints Basil, Jerome, Augustine, and John Chrysostom, made very little linguistic progress; they followed Plato and the Stoics in saying that language was given to men by God, and they devoted most of their efforts to establishing the Christian faith. The Scholastics, however, living in the Middle Ages, when the Church no longer had to fight for survival, had time to revive speculation about language. The famous controversy between the "realists" and the "nominalists" was really a kind of revival of the old Anomalist-Analogist argument. In general, however, the Scholastics adopted Aristotle's views about language. They gave grammar its place in the *trivium* and studied the Latin language intensively. In the Scholastic period we find many treatises on grammar, such as those of St. Anselm and Duns Scotus. The "great school-grammar of the Middle Ages," however, was the *Doctrinale puerorum* of Alexander de Villa-Dei (1199), based on the work of Priscian. [7] This famous grammar and its background we must examine with some care.

---

[6] Charles C. Fries, *The Teaching of the English Language* (New York, Thomas Nelson and Sons, 1927), p. 20.

[7] Gray, *op. cit.*, pp. 426–428.

RISE OF LATIN GRAMMAR

We have already seen, in the first chapter of this book, that for the scholars of the Middle Ages, grammar, as combined in the *trivium* with logic and rhetoric, meant the study of Latin literature as well as of the Latin language; we have also seen that in this period a knowledge of Latin was the first requirement for any kind of learning, since in that language nearly all the available knowledge was to be found. It is easy to see that, as Taylor pointed out, "Men would not at first distinguish sharply between the mediating value of the learned tongue and the learning it held." [8] And perhaps this was fortunate, for the study of grammar kept Latin alive, and hence kept learning alive:

> Had mediaeval Latin failed to keep itself veritable Latin; had it instead suffered transmutation into local Romance dialects, the Latin classics, and all that hung from them, might have become as unknown to the Middle Ages as the Greek, and even have been lost forever. [9]

The grammars of Donatus and Priscian, however, were in some ways inadequate for people whose native languages were not Latin but the vernaculars; moreover, medieval Latin itself came to be very different from classical Latin in matters of syntax, the area in which the Latin grammars written for Romans was, understandably, least definite. Continued, unchecked change would, of course, have made comprehension of the Latin classics difficult, even for those who were in the habit of using medieval Latin in their daily lives:

> Word-forms alone will not preserve the continuity of a language; it is essential that their use in speech and writing should be kept congruous through appropriate principles of syntax. Such were intelligently formulated by medieval grammarians. [10]

[8] Henry Osborn Taylor, *The Mediaeval Mind* (London, Macmillan & Co., Ltd., 1938), Vol. II, p. 361.
[9] *Ibid.*, p. 149.
[10] *Ibid.*, p. 152.

Alexander de Villa-Dei's *Doctrinale* was the most notable attempt to add to the grammars in current use the principles of syntax. This book "for some three hundred years was the common manual of grammatical teaching throughout western Europe." [11] It should be noted that Alexander did not rely entirely upon classical writings in his attempt to set forth rules for syntax; he tried to make his rules conform to the best Latin usage of his time, and he advocated the use of recent Christian as well as classical authors as models in teaching. [12] Those who followed him were not to be so liberal, however.

It is primarily in this period—the twelfth and thirteenth centuries —that grammar became involved with logic:

> Grammar could not help becoming dialectical when the intellectual world was turning to logic and metaphysics. . . . So dialectic brought both good and ill, proving itself helpful in the regulation of syntax, but banefully affecting grammarians with the notion that language was the creature of reason, and must conform to principles of logic. [13]

Some medieval grammarians even advanced the notion that "in order to be a science, grammar must be universal . . . and must possess principles, not applicable specially to Greek or Latin, but to *congruous construction in the abstract*. . . ." [14]

It is thus in this period that the notion of language as absolute and unchanging and of grammar as formal, prescriptive, and quite divorced from usage, has its roots.

Though Latin was the universal language of the Middle Ages, the vernacular languages developed and assumed an ever increasing importance in this period. After the fall of Constantinople in 1453, the Greek revival added new impetus to the study of language, as did the period of exploration which followed: new lands meant new languages for explorer and missionary to learn. [15] By the sixteenth century, grammars of nearly all the vernacular languages had appeared. Most of these were formal grammars, based on the familiar medieval Latin models.

[11] *Ibid.*, p. 153.
[12] *Ibid.*, p. 153.
[13] *Ibid.*, pp. 154–155.
[14] *Ibid.*, p. 155.
[15] Gray, *op. cit.*, p. 428.

We must now examine in some detail the application of this medieval Latin pattern to the study of grammar in English.

REFERENCES

BLOOMFIELD, Leonard, *Introduction to the Study of Language* (New York, Henry Holt and Co., 1914).

FRIES, Charles C., *The Teaching of the English Language* (New York, Thomas Nelson and Sons, 1927).

GRAY, Louis H., *Foundations of Language* (New York, The Macmillan Co., 1939).

TAYLOR, Henry Osborn, *The Mediaeval Mind* (London, Macmillan & Co., Ltd., 1938).

III

The Rise of English Grammar

ONE MAY WONDER how anyone after the time of Chaucer could question the quality of the English language as a medium for literary expression. It is a fact, however, that the quality of English was questioned, and frequently.

It was questioned first of all on the ground that the English vocabulary was inadequate to convey the subtle shades of meaning with which really good writers wished to enrich their work. The printer and translator William Caxton, in the fifteenth century, attempted to remedy this "deficiency" in English by adding to its vocabulary many Latin words. Such attempts to remedy the supposed "poverty" of English gave rise to the "inkhorn" style of writing which was denounced by such Elizabethan writers as Sir John Cheke, Roger Ascham, Thomas Wilson, and Richard Mulcaster. Mulcaster's *The First Part of the Elementary, which Entreateth Chiefly of the Right Writing of our English Tongue* (1582) contains a vigorous defense of English as a medium of expression:

I love Rome, but London better; I favor Italy, but England more; I honor the Latin, but I worship the English. . . . I do not think that any language, be it whatsoever, is better able to utter arguments, either with more pith or greater plainness, than our English tongue is, if the English utterer be as skilful in the matter which he is to utter as the foreign utterer is. [1]

---

[1] Quoted in Albert C. Baugh, ed., *A Literary History of England* (New York, Appleton-Century-Crofts, Inc., 1948), p. 436.

And we find "E.K.," in the epistle to Gabriel Harvey prefixed to Spenser's *Shepheardes Calender* (1579), defending Spenser's use of archaisms and praising him because

He hath laboured to restore, as to their rightful heritage such good and natural English words, as have bene long time out of use and almost cleane disinherited. Which is the onely cause, that our mother tonge, which truly of itself is both ful enough for prose and stately enough for verse, hath long time ben counted most bare and barrein of both. Which default, when as some endevoured to salve and secure, they patched up the holes with peces and rags of other languages . . . So now they have made our English tongue, a gallimaufrey or hodgepodge of al other speeches . . . Whose first shame is, that they are not ashamed, in their own mother tonge straungers to be counted and alienes." [2]

The charge of poverty in vocabulary was made less and less frequently as English literature burgeoned during the reign of Elizabeth.

A second charge replaced the first, however—that English was at best a kind of barbarous growth, greatly in need of polish and of refinement. This idea resulted in many demands in the seventeenth and early eighteenth centuries for an English academy like those which had been established in France and Italy: a partial list of such demands would include those of Edmund Ballon in 1617, Dryden in 1664 and 1679, Evelyn in 1665, Defoe in 1697, Addison in 1711, and Swift in 1712. [3] As we shall see, no such academy was ever established in England.

LATIN GRAMMAR IN ENGLISH

In the meantime, every schoolboy studied his Latin grammar. The methods employed in teaching grammar seem to us very harsh indeed. Roger Ascham, in *The Schoolmaster*, first printed in 1570, attempted to set forth a more humane method. He tells us that he

[2] *The Poetical Works of Edmund Spenser*, p. 417.
[3] Charles C. Fries, *The Teaching of the English Language* (New York, Thomas Nelson and Sons, 1927), p. 22.

was moved to write the book after a conversation with Sir Richard Sackville, who testified that his schoolmaster drove him "with fear of beating from all love of learning." [4] Ascham advocated a system of "double translation"—Latin to English and then English to Latin; he also recommended great discretion in the use of the rod and of harsh reproof in dealing with wayward or slow students. Though he knew Latin and Greek, he wrote his most important books in English and prided himself on having written "English matter in the English tongue for English men." [5]

Ascham had a precedent for using English in teaching. The first Latin grammar in English, that written by William Lyly with the assistance of Colet and Erasmus, had been published perhaps as early as 1513. It went through many editions and revisions, and in 1542 Henry VIII made it the standard text for school use. As a schoolboy, Shakespeare probably studied this grammar, which has been called the most influential of all English textbooks. [6]

Lyly's work is important for English grammar, since it set a standard of arrangement for the material, in that a Latin paradigm with English translation alongside easily suggested that English forms be presented in similar tabulations, with the same terminology as for Latin. [7]

Editions of this book continued to appear until 1858.

Within the next hundred years, a number of grammars of English appeared, most of them having their material arranged like that in Lyly's *Latin Grammar*. In 1568, Thomas Smith published at Paris a work on English written in Latin; in 1580, James Bellot published in London an English grammar for speakers of French; in 1586 William Bullokar published *A Bref Grammar for English*. Other grammars followed: one by John Stockwood in 1590, one by Alexander Gill in 1621, and one by John Hewes in 1624. In

---

[4] Ray Lawson and Smith Hallett, eds., *The Golden Hind: An Anthology of Elizabethan Prose and Poetry* (New York, W. W. Norton and Co., 1942), p. 474.

[5] Baugh, *op. cit.*, p. 333.

[6] *Ibid.*, p. 328.

[7] Roland G. Kent, *Language and Philology* (Boston, Marshall Jones Co., 1923), p. 132.

1634, Charles Butler printed an *English Grammar* using a phonetic alphabet, and in 1640 Simon Daines published a work on English spelling and punctuation. [8] Thanks to Lyly and his followers, it was no longer necessary for students to memorize the rules of grammar *in Latin* before they were allowed to begin reading.

The most important English grammar in this period, however, is Ben Jonson's *The English Grammar*, published in 1640. As has already been pointed out, Jonson's work plainly shows the influence of the Latin grammars. He used the Latin parts of speech, including both substantives and adjectives under the term *noun*, counting the participle as a separate part of speech, and considering articles as pronouns. He said that there were two declensions and six genders of nouns in English and four conjugations of verbs, as in Latin. [9]

By the time Ben Jonson's grammar was published, courses in the reading, writing, and spelling of English had already been added to the curriculum of elementary schools and in some instances to the lower classes of grammar schools. The movement to institute such vernacular studies in elementary education was led by the Bohemian educator Comenius and by Brinsley and Hoole. Brinsley and Hoole both mention the vernacular grammar for "pettie" schools written in 1596 by Edmund Coote as being a text often used for such instruction. This book devoted 32 pages to the teaching of the alphabet and spelling; 18 pages to the catechism, prayers, and psalms; 5 pages to chronology; 2 to writing copies; 2 to arithmetic; and the rest to the explanation of "hard words." [10] Such instruction was regarded as preparation for the study of Latin, the teaching of which was still the primary function of the grammar schools.

Lyman regards John Locke's *Some Thoughts Concerning Education* (1693) as the beginning of the movement to establish the

[8] *Ibid.*, p. 133.
[9] *Ibid.*, pp. 135–136.
[10] Rollo L. Lyman, *English Grammar in American Schools Before 1850*, U. S. Office of Education Bulletin No. 12 (Washington, 1921), pp. 11–13.

study of English grammar, composition, and literature in the colleges and intermediate schools. [11] In this work Locke reopened the attack begun by Mulcaster more than a hundred years earlier on the exclusive study of Latin in the schools. He sought to establish "the principle that for the masses a vernacular education of a secondary grade is equivalent to a Latin education of the same grade for a privileged few." [12] Locke and his followers pointed out that it was folly to teach only Latin to students who would use English almost exclusively in their social and business relationships. This was a practical argument, and many people found it convincing.

Sir Richard Steele, in *The Tatler* (1710), added his support to those who agreed with Locke:

It has been the practice of the wisest nations to learn their own language by stated rules to avoid the confusion that would follow from leaving it to vulgar use. . . . To speak and write without absurdity the language of one's own country is commendable in persons in all stations, and to some indispensably necessary. [13]

Steele's idea that English should be studied in order to improve the standards of speaking and writing was dealt with at some length by Thomas Sheridan in his *British Education; or the Source of the Disorders of Great Britain, being an Essay towards proving, that the Immorality, Ignorance, and false Taste which so generally prevail are the natural and necessary consequences of the present defective System of Education, with An Attempt to show that a Revival of the Art of Speaking, and the Study of our own Language, might contribute, in a Great Measure to the Cure of these Evils* (1756). This book was dedicated to Lord Chesterfield, who was famous as an orator in his own day. Its title indicates very clearly the point of view of its author. [14]

EIGHTEENTH-CENTURY INFLUENCES

The fact that the rise of the middle class in the eighteenth century contributed to the demand for the study of English grammar

[11] *Ibid.*, pp. 11, 13.   [12] *Ibid.*, p. 57.   [13] *Ibid.*, p. 58.   [14] *Ibid.*, p. 55.

we have already noted briefly. As business and trade became more important, English became more important as the language of business and trade; and as prosperity increased for many people, so did leisure for the pursuit of culture, of which correctness in speaking and writing could be assumed to be a part.

It must also be noted that the climate of opinion in the eighteenth century was such as to make a demand for correctness in language almost inevitable. At the risk of oversimplifying, one may say that it was natural for the "Age of Reason" to attempt to apply an absolute standard to language:

Without entering the discussion concerning the relative importance of the various critical creeds and theories of literature and art . . . one can . . . safely conclude that neoclassicism did exist and that there was much discussion of "rules" and "reasons" and "correct writers." [15]

The grammars of the eighteenth century, as Fries points out, were very different from those published in the sixteenth and seventeenth centuries, most of which were intended either for foreigners who wished to learn English, or for those who wished to use English as a tool in the study of Latin. The eighteenth-century grammars, unlike these, "aimed to teach English people correct English." [16] Their authors set out to purify the language and to make it fit the rules of Latin grammar. "They definitely repudiated usage, *even the usage of the best authors*, as the standard of correctness." [17] Wrote James Buchanon in the preface to his *Regular English Syntax* (1767), "Considering the many grammatical Improprieties to be found in our best Writers, such as Swift, Addison, Pope, etc., a Systematical English Syntax is not beneath the Notice of the Learned themselves." [18] And William Ward, in his *English Grammar* (1765), praises Lowth's grammar because of its excellent notes, "in which are shown the grammatic inaccuracies that have escaped the pens of our most distinguished Writers. . . ." [19]

Fries has made a careful examination of 51 English grammars

[15] Fries, *op. cit.*, pp. 24–25.
[16] *Ibid.*, p. 10.
[17] *Ibid.*, pp. 13–14.
[18] *Ibid.*, p. 12.
[19] *Ibid.*, p. 15.

written between 1586 and 1825 in an attempt to determine the purposes and ideas about language of their authors. Of these, 31 grammars were actually written in the eighteenth century, and 26 of the 31 were written after 1750. In these grammars he finds a surprising unanimity of purpose: all of them attempt to reduce the language to rule and to correct usage by making it conform to "reason"; in other words, they "assume a certain accurate, absolute measuring rod of correctness in grammar and repudiate all usage that does not conform to this standard." [20] They also show a surprising unanimity of method: all of these grammars, Fries found, make use of the apparatus of Latin grammar, even those whose authors, like Priestley, do express some qualms as to the value of this system for teaching English. [21]

For our purposes, the most important of these grammars are Robert Lowth's *A Short Introduction to English Grammar* (1762), which was used at Harvard between 1774 and 1841; William Ward's *A Grammar of the English Language* (1765); and Charles Coote's *Elements of the Grammar of the English Language* (1788). These three books are most important as having formed the basis of one of the most influential grammars of the nineteenth century —that written by the American Lindley Murray. His *Grammar of the English Language Adapted to the Different Classes of Learners,* published in 1795, went through some 200 editions and was as influential in England as in America. H. L. Mencken says that "it would not be absurd to argue that [Murray] was responsible beyond all others for the linguistic lag visible in the Mother Country to this day." [22]

Other eighteenth-century grammars by English authors having wide use and influence in both America and England were Thomas Dilworth's *A New Guide to the English Tongue* (1740), which

[20] Charles C. Fries, "The Rules of Common School Grammars," *PMLA,* Vol. XLII, No. 1 (March, 1927), p. 231.
[21] *Ibid.*
[22] Henry L. Mencken, *The American Language,* 4th ed. (New York, Alfred A. Knopf, 1936), p. 101.

was primarily a speller but which had a section devoted to grammar; James Greenwood's *An Essay Towards a Practical English Grammar* (1711); James Harris' *Hermes, or a Philosophical Inquiry Concerning Grammar* (1751); A. Fisher's *Practical New Grammar* (1763), which was used by Goold Brown in writing his *Grammar of Grammars;* and Ash's *Grammatical Institutes* (1763), which was based on Lowth's *English Grammar*. [23] All of these works reflect in general the same philosophy; that is, they present their material in the manner in which Latin grammar was traditionally presented, and they set up rules based upon the rules of Latin grammar or on arbitrary "reason," ignoring usage. [24]

What happened, then, seems to be this: when late in the eighteenth century English finally supplanted Latin in the secondary schools, the methods which had been used to study the dead language, Latin, were simply transferred to the living language, English. As Lyman puts it:

When the Latin grammar school was proved to be ill-suited to the majority of pupils, and when the demand increased for a type of secondary education to supplant the Latin, English grammar came naturally to the fore. Instruction in vernacular grammar could be imparted by exactly the same methods used in the teaching of Latin grammar. The passing of Latin grammar is contemporaneous with the rise of vernacular grammar. The older order—reading, writing, spelling, and Latin grammar—now became reading, writing, spelling, English grammar, all in the Mother Tongue. [25]

The eighteenth-century grammarians took upon themselves the task of making English fit the Latin pattern.

It may be pointed out, in summary, that there were three factors in the growth of the demand for correctness which these grammarians attempted to meet: the notion that English was a barbarous language sadly in need of reform; the rise of the middle class; and the eighteenth-century climate of opinion, which led men to seek,

[23] Lyman, *op. cit.,* pp. 33–35.
[24] Fries, "The Rules of Common School Grammars," pp. 226–232.
[25] Lyman, *op. cit.,* p. 20.

in nearly every aspect of life, for "rule" and "reason." [26] It may also be pointed out again that this artificial prescriptive grammar, the result of circumstances peculiar to the eighteenth century, is the basis of the formal grammar taught in the nineteenth century and still being taught in many of our schools.

REFERENCES

BAUGH, Albert C., ed., *A Literary History of England* (New York, Appleton-Century-Crofts, Inc., 1948).

FRIES, Charles C., "The Rules of Common School Grammars," *PMLA*, Vol. XLII, No. 1 (March, 1927).

FRIES, Charles C., *The Teaching of the English Language* (New York, Thomas Nelson and Sons, 1927).

KENT, Roland G., *Language and Philology* (Boston, Marshall Jones Co., 1923).

LAWSON, Ray, and HALLETT, Smith, eds., *The Golden Hind: An Anthology of Elizabethan Prose and Poetry* (New York, W. W. Norton and Co., 1942).

LYMAN, Rollo L., *English Grammar in American Schools Before 1850*, U. S. Office of Education Bulletin No. 12 (Washington, 1921).

MENCKEN, Henry L., *The American Language*, 4th ed. (New York, Alfred A. Knopf, 1936).

[26] Fries, *The Teaching of the English Language*, pp. 21–25.

IV

English Grammar in the United States Before 1900

EIGHTEENTH-CENTURY ATTITUDES toward language and grammar as developed in England almost completely dominated the teaching of grammar in the United States until the close of the nineteenth century and set a pattern which persists to the present. It is both interesting and revealing to trace out the channels of this influence and to examine some of its practical results in the preparation, publication, and classroom use of grammar books.

It has been shown in the previous chapter that the rise of grammar as a corrective device for the improvement of English is a product of the eighteenth century, and more particularly of the latter half of that century: "Whereas fewer than fifty writings on grammar, rhetoric, criticism and linguistic theory have been listed for the first half of the eighteenth century . . . the publications in the period 1750–1800 exceeded 200 titles." [1] Nearly all of these works were concerned with propriety and correctness in the use of English. Long tradition had established the axiom that "correct" Latin was engendered by the grammar of Latin; it was natural to think that "correct" English would be engendered by English grammars, and if none suitable were at hand, they could be created for the purpose. It was equally natural that the grammars so cre-

[1] Sterling A. Leonard, *The Doctrine of Correctness in English Usage, 1700–1800*, University of Wisconsin Studies in Language and Literature, No. 25 (Madison, Wis., 1929), p. 12.

ated should reflect the traditional patterns of Latin grammar, a Procrustean bed to fit which the grammatical patterns of English were chopped and stretched.

It is a fact of considerable significance that the prescriptive development of English grammar was taking place in England at the same time that private and public education were expanding on this side of the Atlantic. Lyman says, "We are safe in saying not only that the American colonists inherited from England the grammar school and college, but that they endeavored to go beyond the mother country in teaching the vernacular." [2] But with the shift to English grammar from the Latin, there was little change in the theory and practice of teaching. Lyman continues:

In the Latin school the backbone of the course had been grammar; the term *grammar*, the method of teaching grammar were ingrained. Latin grammar had stood for the next step above reading and writing the vernacular ... when, therefore, the advocates of a practical English training [in the American colonies] found English grammar in Dilworth and other texts, what was more natural than that they would seize upon it as a suitable substitute for the next step above reading and writing and spelling? English they found reduced to the same accidence as Latin; textbooks informed them on title pages that grammar was the art of speaking and writing the English language correctly, and this was their laudable desire for their children; here is a suitable setting in the vernacular program for grammar as the basic study. This conviction made its way into legal sanction for English and English grammar in the last decade of the eighteenth century. [3]

From the evidence of Lyman and others it appears that the decade 1750–60 is the period in which English grammar began to make its way into the curriculums of American colonial schools, and that only a scattering of secondary schools did much with grammar until 1775. With the rapid development of the theory of public education for all in the last part of the eighteenth century, English grammar moved into the position of a basic study. "The

[2] Rollo L. Lyman, *English Grammar in American Schools Before 1850*, U. S. Office of Education Bulletin No. 12 (Washington, 1921), p. 17.
[3] *Ibid.*, pp. 76, 77.

period immediately after the Revolution marks the well-nigh universal adoption of English into the curricula of American schools." [4] From these beginnings, grammar retained its central place in upper elementary and secondary education through the nineteenth century.

ENGLISH TEXTBOOKS IN AMERICA

At first the colonies turned to England for textbooks in the new subject. Some twelve English grammars appear to have been imported for use in the schools, only three of which attained great popularity: Dilworth's *A New Guide to the English Tongue* (London, 1740), Lowth's *A Short Introduction to English Grammar* (London, 1758), and an anonymous *British Grammar* (London, 1760). Of these, that of Lowth had the greatest influence on American schools, inasmuch as Lindley Murray copied most of his rules from Lowth and was in turn copied by numerous imitators.

These grammar books were not only imported but were reprinted for sale in the colonies. Dilworth was reprinted as early as 1747, Lowth in 1775, and the anonymous *British Grammar* in 1784. [5] Less widely used but of early appearance were the English grammars of American authors. "The first English grammar by an American was written in 1724 by Hugh Jones, professor of mathematics in William and Mary." [6] The first grammar written and published in the colonies seems to be that of Samuel Johnson, the first president of Kings College (now Columbia University), who offered in 1765 *The First Easy Rudiments of Grammar, applied to the English Tongue*. Noah Webster's *A Grammatical Institute of the English Language*, published in Hartford, 1784, is sometimes erroneously called the first American English grammar, perhaps because in time it became the most widely used of the

[4] *Ibid.*, p. 70.   [5] *Ibid.*, p. 34.   [6] *Ibid.*, p. 32.

grammars of the late eighteenth century, with the exception of Lindley Murray's.

Three influences at the close of the eighteenth century stimulated the importance given to training in English and hence the use of English grammars. One was the great amount of public speaking engaged in at the time, a natural concomitant of the furious political activity. Public speech called for polished style; polished style rested on rules; the grammars furnished the rules. The second influence was the absorption of large numbers of non-English-speaking people, who in learning English tended to blend its grammar with their own as well as to retain words and idioms merely transliterated into English. To curb this corruptive influence the schools felt the need of a fixed standard in English, eagerly turning to the rules of the grammar books as a providential authority. The third influence was a feeling of social, literary, and educational insecurity. Among a pioneer people, occupied with the task of producing the material necessities of life in a virgin territory, it is natural to incline toward established authority in cultural matters. This cultural dependence of the American colonies is clearly seen in the arts, in literature, and in their attitudes toward standards of language usage.

With Webster's *Plain and Comprehensive Grammar* of 1784 a shower of textbooks in grammar began to fall on the American schools. Seventeen other books appeared before 1795. [7] In that year Lindley Murray's *English Grammar, Adapted to the Different Classes of Learners,* made its appearance. This book, together with his *Abridgement* (1797), *An English Grammar, in Two Volumes* (1814), and *English Exercises* (1802), reached a total of over 120 editions of 10,000 copies each, so that more than 1,000,000 copies of his books were sold in America before 1850. Adding to this total the sales of his imitators yields a grand total of something over 2,000,000 copies. Since Murray copied extensively from Lowth, here is abundant evidence of the establishment of eighteenth-cen-

[7] *Ibid.,* p. 78.

tury prescriptive grammar in the schoolbooks of the United States from 1795 to 1850 and beyond.

In the first decades of the new century, four more texts appeared which gained enormous popularity, gradually superseding Webster and Murray. These were Samuel Kirkham's *English Grammar in Familiar Lectures* (1825), Goold Brown's *Grammatical Institutes* (1825), Peter Bullion's *Principles of English Grammar* (1834), and Roswell Smith's two grammars of 1829 and 1831. "Smith's grammars were used more than all others combined in Massachusetts during these decades. Bullion, Brown, Smith, and Kirkham divided the grammatical field of New York about evenly among them." [8] Toward the close of the first half of the century, three more texts appeared which had considerable influence. William H. Wells published his *School Grammar* in 1846, Samuel S. Greene's *The Analysis of Sentences* came the next year, and in 1851 Goold Brown brought out his colossal *Grammar of Grammars*. This latter work was the epitome of the eighteenth-century tradition. In its more than a thousand pages of fine print the student found rules to memorize, exercises to parse, and quotations from standard authors to "correct." Brown says himself that this is the traditional method, "I mean, especially the ancient positive method, which aims directly at the inculcation of principles." [9] The *Grammar of Grammars* marked the pinnacle and decline of the traditional concept of language and grammar as derived from the eighteenth century. Tendencies already visible in earlier grammars became more and more pronounced, so that by the third quarter of the century a new theory of grammar was superseding the old, bringing with it a new attitude toward language itself. Yet with the changes in theory, much of the specific subject matter remained unchanged, appearing in text after text even to the present day, carried along by the weight of tradition. [10]

[8] *Ibid.*, p. 133, footnote.
[9] Goold Brown, *Grammar of English Grammars* (New York, 1851), p. 86.
[10] For detailed evidence of this point, see Robert C. Pooley, *Grammar and Usage in Textbooks on English*, Bulletin 14, University of Wisconsin Bureau of Educational Research (Madison, Wis., 1933), Chs. IV, V, and VI.

POINT OF VIEW OF EARLY GRAMMARS

It is now time to examine what these grammars have to say about their purpose for being and their relationship to the use of English. Typical of the position of the eighteenth-century English grammars is this statement from the preface to Buchanon's grammar of 1767:

> Considering the many grammatical Improprieties to be found in our best Writers, such as Swift, Addison, Pope, etc. a Systematical English syntax is not beneath the Notice of the Learned themselves. Should it be urged, that in the time of these writers, English was but very little subjected to Grammar, that they had scarcely a single Rule to direct them, a question readily occurs. Had they not the Rules of Latin Syntax to direct them? [11]

Here we see unmistakably the corrective principle and its source. Even the greatest of English authors made "mistakes" because they had no rules to guide them; but lacking rules, why did they not derive them from Latin grammar, with which they were naturally all acquainted? Webster in his grammar of 1807 says, paralleling the position of his forerunners, "There are many grammatical errors in the writers of the 16th and 17th centuries, which Lowth, Priestly, Blair, and Campbell have enumerated in their respective works, and many of them are copied into Murray's grammar."

Samuel Kirkham is distressed by the imperfections of English, which grammar can correct:

> In the grammar of the perfect language, no rules should be admitted, but such as are founded on fixed principles, arising out of the genius of that language and the nature of things; but our language being *im*-perfect, it becomes necessary, in a practical treatise, like this, to adopt some rules to direct us in the use of speech as regulated by *Custom*. If we had a permanent and surer standard than capricious custom to regulate us in the transmission of thought, great inconvenience would be avoided. They, however, who introduce usages which depart from

[11] Charles C. Fries, "The Rules of the Common School Grammars," *PMLA*, Vol. XLII, No. 1 (March, 1927), p. 232.

the analogy and philosophy of a language, are conspicuous among the number of those who form that language. [12]

Kirkham sighs over the imperfections of English, many of which he feels are introduced by, or given currency by, the great English writers, who ought to know better.

Peter Bullion finds comfort in the regulating influence of grammar. He says:

Prior to the publication of Lowth's excellent little grammar, the grammatical study of our own language formed no part of the ordinary method of instruction, and consequently the writings of the best authors were frequently inaccurate. Subsequent to that period, however, attention has been paid to this important subject, and the change that has taken place both in our written and oral language, has evidenced the decided advantages resulting from such a plan. [13]

Although Goold Brown's first grammar was published in 1823, discussion of it has been deferred in order to include at the same time his monumental *Grammar of Grammars* of 1851. In the twenty-eight years of interval there is no change in his point of view; the latter is only an enormous elaboration of the principles expressed in the former. There seems to be no injustice, therefore, in placing side by side excerpts from the two works to exhibit Goold Brown's position.

The author of the *Institutes* reveals himself as a static grammarian; he sees language as a fixed entity, perfect in theory, but still hampered by impurities which it is the duty of the grammarian to eradicate. He says, "Hence the need that an able and discreet grammarian should now and then appear, who with skillful hand can effect those corrections which a change of fashion or the ignorance of authors may have made necessary"; that he is such a grammarian he has no doubt. [14] Usage he finds dangerous; it is by no means a safe guide to correctness. "Etymology and custom are seldom at

[12] Samuel Kirkham, *English Grammar in Familiar Lectures*, 11th ed. (Rochester, N. Y., 1830), p. 18.
[13] Peter Bullion, *Principles of English Grammar* (New York, 1844), pp. 189, 190.
[14] Brown, *op. cit.*, p. 10.

odds and where they are so, the latter can hardly be deemed infallible." [15] Usage, he protests is not a safe guide, but the rules of a master grammarian may be relied upon, memorized, and applied ever afterwards. His plan of teaching is in perfect accord with this theory. "The only successful method of teaching grammar is to cause the principal definitions and rules to be committed thoroughly to memory, that they may ever afterwards be readily applied." [16] In this way English will become fixed, regular, and pure. The idea of future change and growth does not form part of Brown's theory. The grammarian, he says, "presumes to be a *judge of authorship*, and a *teacher of teachers*." [17] Such a grammarian will find that though authors claim the authority of good use,

No few have departed from it, even while they were pretending to record its dictates. . . . Nay, while new blunders have been committed in every new book, old ones have been allowed to stand as by prescriptive right; and positions that were never true, and sentences that were never good English, have been published, and republished under different names, until in our language, grammar has become the most ungrammatical of all studies. [18]

Into this unhappy situation Brown arrives as the messiah to lead the way to a correct and perfect grammar. Nor does he spare his predecessors and contemporaries. Webster has dared to set up custom over authority: "What marvel, then, that all his multifarious grammars of the English language are despised?" [19] Murray was a *"professed compiler;* who had so mean an opinion of what his theme required, as to deny it even the common courtesies of compilation!" [20] Murray's successors wrote "works of little or no merit. . . . It is comical to see what they say in their prefaces." Upon Kirkham he bestows a galling pity: "It is cruel in any man to look narrowly into the faults of an author who peddles a school book for bread. . . . Far be it from me to notice any such character, ex-

[15] *Ibid.*
[16] Goold Brown, *The Institutes of English Grammar* (New York, 1825), preface.
[17] Brown, *Grammar of English Grammars*, p. 10.
[18] *Ibid.*, p. 11.　　　[19] *Ibid.*, p. 14.　　　[20] *Ibid.*

cept with kindness and charity." [21] The title to Greene's grammar is a "libel and a lie"; Smith's grammar "is a grammatical chaos." Having thus cleared the way, Brown modestly concludes, "A grammar should speak for itself. . . . The merit of casting up a highway in a rugged land, is proportionate not merely to the utility of the achievement but to the magnitude of the obstacles to be overcome . . . the author . . . has voluntarily pursued the study, with an assiduity which no man will ever imitate for the sake of pecuniary recompense." [22]

The influence of Brown, great as it was, was not destined to flourish unchallenged. His theory and method of teaching grammar were even in 1851 somewhat reactionary; already Smith, with his insistence on the sentence as the foundation of grammar and his scheme for the inductive teaching of grammar, was pointing the way that grammar instruction was to go. Brown knew of these changes and derided them. He was in the wrong, however; the same spirit in education which was substituting the field trip for the botany book, the laboratory for the chemistry book, and the observatory for the formal astronomy book was to turn the attention of students to the language itself as the source of rule and method. This change, however, though its signs were apparent in the second quarter of the nineteenth century, was exceedingly slow of accomplishment. It is by no means completed yet, for notwithstanding great advances in theory, the force of tradition has been strong, causing rule after rule to be copied from book to book, frequently affording the critical reader amusing comparisons between the affirmations of the preface and the actualities of the text itself. The spirit of Goold Brown has not yet been laid to rest.

SIGNS OF CHANGE

Samuel S. Greene, upon whom the wrath of Brown fell, was one of the pioneers in the new attitude toward the teaching of gram-

[21] *Ibid.*, p. 28.   [22] *Ibid.*, p. 99.

mar. He omits from his work the eighteenth-century philosphical views of grammar as Universal and Particular, he fails to copy the often-quoted doctrine of usage of Campbell, and (most significant) he offers no quotations from authors for correction. On the other hand, he stresses *doing* as necessary to learning, and in this anticipates the "functional" grammars of the early twentieth century. He says, ". . . it is believed that children perceive grammatical . . . relations more easily from what they have to perform, than from what they have to commit to memory." [23] Quite consistently he stresses the sentence as the foundation of English grammar, building up from the sentence and its parts a comprehensive view of grammar.

The story of grammar teaching in the second half of the nineteenth century is, in the field of theory, the battle of the functionalists, successors to Greene, against the forces of authority, successors to Brown. From the large volume of evidence of the struggle, a few brief quotations will serve to illustrate the battle. In 1870 R. G. White published a book on the theory of language in which he revived all the eighteenth-century watchwords: logic, reason, analogy, natural and universal grammar, and strong opposition to custom. He says,

Speech, the product of reason, tends more and more to conform itself to reason; and when grammar, which is the formulation of usage, is opposed to reason, there arises, sooner or later, a conflict between logic, or the law of reason, and grammar, the law of precedent, in which the former is always victorious. Usage . . . is not . . . the absolute law of language. . . . There is a misuse of words which can be justified by no authority, however great, by no usage, however general. [24]

This theory of the relationship of grammar to language has by no means been vanquished at the present time, and it forms the bulwark of those contemporary teachers who for one reason or

---

[23] Samuel Greene, *First Lessons in Grammar* (Philadelphia, 1848), preface.
[24] R. G. White, *Words and Their Uses*, new ed. (New York, 1872), pp. 23, 24.

another are unable or unwilling to accept the attitude toward language and grammar developed by linguistic science.

One of White's leading opponents was Fitzedward Hall, who published in 1872 and 1873 two works attacking White's theories by piling up example after example of literary usage invalidating White's strictures and revealing with considerable glee the all-too-apparent errors in scholarship of which White had been guilty. He answers White thus:

Now, by usage of speech we mean the forms of it which are customarily employed; and by grammar and lexicography, orderly records thereof. Although, then, speech tended "more and more to conform itself to reason" grammar could never be opposed to reason; since, as speech changes, itself changes. . . . The case standing thus, how is it that Mr. White wishes to revive English which has become obsolete, and how it is that he is so sorely grieved by the English of his contemporaries, may well perplex us." [25]

The essential conflict is whether the grammarian by the use of reason and by reference to the "genius" of the language is empowered to create rules for the governing of English regardless of what custom may have developed, or whether the language itself, as it is used by its speakers, is the sole authority for the drawing of "rules" which are in actuality only generalized observations of current practice. From the former point of view is derived the idea that changes in language are corruptions to be corrected; from the latter comes the idea that change is normal and inevitable and that the student of language accurately observes and records the changes.

An early expression of the latter view is to be found in a book of Lounsbury's which was published in 1879. His summary has a surprisingly modern sound:

. . . the history of language, when looked at from the purely grammatical point of view, is little less than the history of corruptions. . . . But it is equally true that these grammatical changes, or corruptions . . .

[25] Fitzedward Hall, *Recent Exemplifications of False Philosophy* (New York, 1872), pp. 66, 88.

have had no injurious effects upon the development of language. . . .
It is, at the present time, a fashion to talk of our speech as being in some
way less pure and vigorous than it was in the days of Alfred. . . . But
the test of any tongue is not the grammatical or linguistic resources
which it may be supposed to possess; it is the use which it makes of
the resources it does possess . . . for it is a lesson which many learn
with difficulty, and some never learn at all, that purism is not purity. [26]

REFERENCES

BROWN, Goold, *Grammar of English Grammars* (New York, 1851).

BROWN, Goold, *The Institutes of English Grammar* (New York, 1825).

BULLION, Peter, *Principles of English Grammar* (New York, 1844).

FRIES, Charles C., "The Rules of the Common School Grammars,"
PMLA, Vol. XLII, No. 1 (March, 1927).

GREENE, Samuel, *First Lessons in Grammar* (Philadelphia, 1848).

HALL, Fitzedward, *Recent Exemplifications of False Philology* (New
York, 1872).

KIRKHAM, Samuel, *English Grammar in Familiar Lectures*, 11th ed.
(Rochester, N. Y., 1830).

LEONARD, Sterling A., *The Doctrine of Correctness in English Usage,
1700–1800*, University of Wisconsin Studies in Language and Literature, No. 25 (Madison, Wis., 1929).

LOUNSBURY, T. R., *History of the English Language* (New York, 1879).

LYMAN, Rollo L., "English Grammar in American Schools Before
1850," U. S. Office of Education Bulletin No. 12 (Washington,
D. C., 1921).

POOLEY, Robert C., *Grammar and Usage in Textbooks on English*, Bulletin No. 14, University of Wisconsin Bureau of Educational Research (Madison, Wis., 1933).

WHITE, R. G., *Words and Their Uses*, new ed. (New York, 1872).

[26] T. R. Lounsbury, *History of the English Language* (New York, 1879),
pp. 351–353.

V

Grammar in Today's Schools

THE PURPOSE OF THIS CHAPTER is to present as factually and realistically as possible the exact state of the teaching of grammar in the public and private schools of the United States in the decade terminating in 1956. It is granted at the outset that every conceivable pattern of grammar teaching can be found, from no grammar at all to the most complete content imaginable. In grade placement the same variety will be found. Some children in the second and third grades are being taught grammatical terminology and functions which for others are reserved to the ninth or tenth grades, or are perhaps completely omitted. Yet with all this ungoverned variety, there is a sort of general point of view and practice, an average content and method, which will provide the experience with grammar for the majority of the children and youth currently in school. To determine this general practice in the teaching of grammar is the goal of this chapter.

No one would seriously question the statement that in the teaching of English there is a considerable lag in practice behind the findings of research and the recommendations of expert teachers. The great majority of teachers tend to continue teaching what they have been taught, and by the same methods. At the same time there will be a progressive minority struggling to establish new ways, accomplish new goals, arrive at better results. What is the situation in grammar in our schools today? To what extent do the practice and content of past years dominate the present? Answers

33

to this question will be sought in research studies, textbooks, courses of study, articles in educational journals, and the opinions of current leaders in English teaching.

Professor Walcott of the University of Michigan has stated the problem and the situation in these words:

> Within the subject of English—as in all other subjects, I would suppose—certain illusions have persisted for nearly half a century despite a good body of reputable research to disprove them. One of these illusions is the supposed efficacy of grammar in improving oral and written composition and in preparing pupils for college. In visiting English classrooms and talking with teachers of English, one is impressed with the persistence of their faith in a knowledge of formal grammar and in the drill-book exercise by which formal rules are supposedly applied automatically to the self-expression of the pupils. One is impressed, too, by the extent to which this formal learning and formal drill still dominate the classroom activity, and still supplant the true exercise of the self-expression to which they are supposed to contribute. In my own frequent visits to English classrooms I am amazed at the extent to which pupils are engaged with the workbook and at the infrequency with which I find them actually practicing self-expression (writing, speaking, conversing, listening to each other, and replying). When I protest mildly my lack of faith in the formal drill, the teacher is likely to express surprise or to remark that surely this is what the colleges want: correct usage and a knowledge of what is right and wrong. My reflection is: Yes, that is what the colleges want all right, but all of our research on the subject proves that these are not the means for securing that kind of ability. [1]

After citing the results of a number of research studies, Walcott concludes, "Teachers apparently persist in the illusions which these very researches should long ago have dispelled."[2] Evidence from several contributing sources supports the conclusion that faith in the efficacy of formal grammar to develop successful writers and speakers is held by a very large number, possibly the majority, of current teachers of English.

[1] Fred G. Walcott, "The Limitations of Grammar," *School of Education Bulletin*, University of Michigan, Vol. 19, No. 4 (January, 1948), p. 49.
[2] *Ibid.*, p. 51.

THE EVIDENCE OF INVESTIGATIONS

In a comprehensive survey of the teaching of English in rural and city schools in the State of Wisconsin, two investigators analyzed approximately 120 lessons in grammar and usage observed in elementary schools including grades seven and eight. The evidence of this survey is that grammar is taught chiefly by rule and by formal exercise the intent of which is to establish improved usage. These authors conclude,

It will be observed that the grammatical elements receiving instructional time cover virtually the whole range of grammar, no marked emphasis being placed on any of them. The weakness of grammar instruction in Wisconsin (and probably in other states) is that so many new concepts and principles are introduced into the sixth, seventh, and eighth grades that pupils find it difficult to grasp them, let alone remember them. . . . To introduce phrases, clauses, and infinitives to such bewildered children seems idiotic, yet the evidence shows that these items are taught in grades seven and eight. [3]

The same investigation shows that usage in the elementary grades was taught by drill and exercises from books. "In rural schools 36 per cent of the lessons consist of workbook practice, and 16 per cent of textbook practice. In city schools the filling-in exercises comprise 24 per cent of the lessons and textbook drills 38 per cent. . . . Original exercises—that is, the pupil's application of a rule or principle to *his own sentences*—occupy only 4 per cent of rural time and 8 per cent of city time. [4]

For the senior high school the Wisconsin survey reveals a similar formalization of grammar instruction. Grammar was defended by teachers chiefly for its supposed influence on correct usage. Grammar as revealing the structure of English was barely recognized. In the specific grammar lessons observed in junior and senior high schools, 82 lessons in all, the breakdown of materials taught is as follows:

[3] Robert C. Pooley and Robert D. Williams, *The Teaching of English in Wisconsin* (Madison, The University of Wisconsin Press, 1948), pp. 79, 80.
[4] *Ibid.*, pp. 76, 77.

CATEGORY OF GRAMMAR	PERCENTAGE OF LESSONS IN		
	Grades 7 & 8	Grades 9–12	All Grades
Analysis and terminology: parts of speech, etc.	87	58	67
Morphology (forms of noun, pronoun, and verb).......	16	17	17
Usage (correctness)	25	34	32
Practice in manipulating elements of the sentence ...	4	13	11
(Some lessons contained more than one category)			

"Analysis and terminology, it will be seen, is the predominant activity." [5] In the methods used to teach the grammar analyzed above, the investigators found that teachers relied largely upon the organization and content of the textbooks in use and made little effort to apply the material to the language needs of individual students. [6] This is reflected in the small amount of time given to the manipulation of elements of the sentence as shown in the table above.

The English teachers of the State of Georgia undertook a similar survey of the teaching of English. The investigators personally visited large numbers of classrooms in the elementary grades, the junior high school, and the senior high school. One purpose of the investigation was to answer the question, When teachers are teaching English, what do they do? As might be expected, lessons in grammar and usage led the total number. Out of 528 lessons observed in grades one to seven, 149 were in grammar and usage, 101 in reading. The remainder were scattered among spelling, mechanics, oral English, writing, literature, and vocabulary. When teachers were asked to rank these instructional items in order of importance, the teachers of the seventh grade ranked reading first, grammar and usage second. Those of the eighth grade ranked literature first, grammar and usage second. Teaching the facts of English grammar

[5] Ibid., p. 162.
[6] Ibid., p. 163.

and usage apparently rates higher than performing the activities of English, such as writing and speaking. [7]

In the high school grades, similar attention to the formal aspects of English was found. "The high school teacher of English in Georgia seems to spend the greater part of her time on grammar and usage and on reading and literature . . . a few teachers spend more than 65 per cent of the teaching time on grammar and usage." In the analysis of time allotment to the various aspects of teaching English in high schools, grammar and usage was first in rank, with a median of 21 to 25 per cent of the total time. "Pupils usually get their heaviest doses of grammar and usage in the seventh grade, slightly less in grades 8–10, considerably less in the eleventh grade, and least in the twelfth. Whether reduction in dosage is due to the progressive cure of the patient or to the despair of the doctor is uncertain." [8]

THE EVIDENCE FROM THE *ENGLISH JOURNAL*

To sample the point of view of teachers currently writing about English grammar, all articles on the subject from January, 1953, to November, 1956, were read and classified. Fourteen articles are included below. These articles fall quite easily into two general categories: (*a*) those which discuss the teaching of grammar from the point of view of attitude and trends; and (*b*) those which describe or evaluate specific methods and procedures in teaching grammar.

Among the articles dealing with trends perhaps the broadest in scope is that of W. Wilbur Hatfield. [9] In response to a controversial book by Professor Warfel,[10] Hatfield sets forth what seem to him to be the basic issues in the consideration of grammar as a part of English instruction in the high school. These six points, he avers, require consideration or exploration:

[7] Paul Farmer and Bernice Freeman, *The Teaching of English in Georgia* (Atlanta, Georgia Council of Teachers of English, 1952), p. 10.

[8] *Ibid.*, pp. 18, 19.

[9] "A Confused Issue," *English Journal*, Vol. XLII, No. 2 (February, 1953), pp. 91, 92.

[10] *Who Killed Grammar?* (Gainesville, University of Florida Press, 1952).

1. Find the reasons why conventional grammar teaching does **not** develop usable concepts.
2. Explore the effectiveness of slower, cumulative methods of instruction.
3. Retest those experiments which claim greater success through direct instruction of specific usages.
4. Discover by research the age at which grammatical concepts **can** be readily learned.
5. To what extent can grammar be learned inductively?
6. What standards of usage should be set for school English?

Hatfield's position is that the "confused issue" is lightened by little solid knowledge; the current opinions, while vehemently expressed, rest upon a weak foundation of fact.

Another critic of divergent views is A. J. Walker, [11] who contrasts the point of view expressed in *Leave Your Language Alone* (see bibliography) with the point of view of formal grammarians. After a careful analysis he concludes that both positions are in error. "I part company with the proponents of more formal grammar because I think it is unrealistic in its approach to the problem and because it simply does not do the job of producing good writing and speaking."

In similar vein Richard M. Bassone criticizes formal grammar: [12]

Today many English teachers, on the assumption that teaching grammar teaches ordered thinking, erroneously reason that in their teaching of the parts of speech and Latin grammatical terminology they are teaching grammar, therefore ordered thinking and meanings. . . . Unfortunately these misunderstandings are the things which have taken us further away from our main goal, which is to help the student grow in ability to think rationally.

Another writer [13] attempts to summarize the status of grammar teaching as of that date and finds little reflection of the work of

[11] "What Language Shall We Teach?" *English Journal*, Vol. XLII, No. 8 (November, 1953), pp. 431–436.
[12] "Let's Talk Sense About English," *English Journal*, Vol. XLIII, No. 7 (October, 1954), pp. 371–373.
[13] Robert C. Pooley, "Grammar in the Schools of Today," *English Journal*, Vol. XLIII, No. 3 (March, 1954), pp. 142–146.

linguistic scholars in current grammar teaching. His principal statement, "the teaching of grammar as a part of English instruction in elementary and high schools has not changed greatly in the last ten years and shows no sign at the moment of rapid change in the years immediately ahead," was picked up by Mary Wood Dawson. She says, "When I read Robert Pooley's statement [that quoted above] I was discouraged by the prophecy."[14] To test the assertion, she made a comparison of the method of teaching pronouns in 21 texts used in the 1920's and 24 texts used in the 1940's. Her findings reveal little change in nomenclature, small regard for the informal uses of pronouns, slight changes in drills, some increase in the use of auditory exercises. She concludes, "This survey on pronouns revealed that the study of grammar still seems to be considered an end in itself rather than the means to the end of correct usage. . . . It seems obvious that textbook authors have not caught up with recent trends which should be presented in textbooks."

The larger number of articles on grammar in the *English Journal* from January, 1953, to November, 1956, were presentations of various ideas and methods in teaching grammar. Without exception these articles point to the functional and realistic uses of grammar as contrasted with traditional and formalized uses of grammar. Donald Cain says, "I found long ago that the rigid formulas (of grammar and sentence structure) of the standard high school texts were so far out of date and so narrow-minded that I could not teach or work by them." [15] As a solution he created sentences involving problems of usage and clarity and allowed his students to solve them as problems, accepting all valid solutions. Similarly Lester Vander Werf places his emphasis upon writing and reports. "The best results [in grammar] were achieved when we relied on grammar not at all, but rather on the stuff itself. . . . Why English teachers persist in going through the same meaningless motions

[14] "The Passing of the Pronoun," *English Journal*, Vol. XLV, No. 1 (January, 1956), pp. 34–37.
[15] "A Sentence Exercise Technique," *English Journal*, Vol. XLIII, No. 6 (September, 1954), pp. 313–315, 319.

without results and without asking why is simply incomprehensible." [16]

Harry K. Hutton warns teachers of the danger in teaching words as grammar. [17] Words are parts of speech, he insists, only as they are used in sentences. Hence the definitions and illustrations of parts of speech can be determined only by the position and function of words in sentences.

The combining of grammar and literature is recommended by M. D. McElroy, [18] who favors the study of function in its setting of use, as in reading materials. His emphasis, however, is more upon the mechanics of English than upon the recognition and understanding of sentence structure.

Great emphasis upon writing as the method of grammar teaching is made by Lorraine D. Sundal, who presents a plan of five steps in the teaching of grammar: [19]

1. Give diagnostic tests to determine present knowledge.
2. Teach structure from the analysis of student writings.
3. Have students analyze their own sentences.
4. Keep all writings in a folder file for constant use by students.
5. Continue diagnosis to reveal growth in knowledge and skill.

In defending grammar as a part of a core program, Reef Waldrep says, "The teacher, with a broader background, should represent not the hidebound rules of a textbook but the generally accepted language of educated Americans." [20] He stresses the use of projects to raise interest in language instruction and diagramming as a skill, without making clear for what purpose the diagramming is intended.

[16] "Are English Teachers Afraid?" *English Journal*, Vol. XLIII, No. 6 (September, 1954), pp. 321, 322.
[17] "Basic Trouble in Teaching Grammar," *English Journal*, Vol. XLIII, No. 6 (September, 1954), p. 320.
[18] "Let the Grammar Grow," *English Journal*, Vol. XLIII, No. 3 (March, 1954), pp. 151–153.
[19] "A Transition Program in Grammar and Usage," *English Journal*, Vol. XLV, No. 4 (April, 1956), pp. 195–200.
English Journal, Vol XLII, No 1 (January, 1953), pp. 24–28.
[20] "Core Teaching Has Plenty of Room for Grammar," *English Journal*, Vol. XLII, No. 1 (January, 1953), pp. 24–28.

Other articles in the *English Journal* deal with various applications of grammar to classroom situations. [21] Mosley advocates the use of students' own sentences for practice in grammar; Strom makes a study of the relation of grammar to reading and concludes that except for students in special classes emphasizing grammar in written and oral expression, there is little connection between the two as ordinarily taught; and Makey reviews the use of diagramming as a teaching device with approval, but without clear reason for the sentence analysis accomplished by the diagrams.

From these articles certain conclusions may be drawn. First, it is evident that teachers writing on grammar in the current *English Journal* are progressive in attitude. They are on the whole functionally minded, desiring to place grammar and its teaching in a setting of utility. They favor direct applications of grammar to writing, and the learning of grammar from writing. Many of them protest what they feel to be a meaningless repetition of traditional methods and rules in grammar, which fail to yield satisfactory results.

THE EVIDENCE FROM COURSES OF STUDY

No attempt will be made here at a thoroughgoing analysis of many courses of study at elementary, junior high school, and senior high school levels. The single point of this section is to find an answer to the question, Is structural grammar still widely taught in the elementary school up to and including grade six? The answer seems to be, yes, much structural grammar is recommended in grades three to six, with a considerable part of the total grammar of English required of students in the sixth grade.

The Elementary Course of Study for the State of Pennsylvania [22]

[21] Lorraine A. Mosley, "Integrated Grammar and Usage," Vol. XLIV, No. 5 (May, 1956), pp. 274, 275; Ingrid M. Strom, "Does Knowledge of Grammar Improve Reading?" Vol. XLV, No. 3 (March, 1956), pp. 129–133; Herman O. Makey, "A Means or an End?" Vol. XLII, No. 3 (March, 1953), pp. 159–160.

[22] Commonwealth of Pennsylvania, Department of Public Instruction, *Bulletin 233B* (Harrisburg, 1949).

offers the following recommendations for the teaching of grammar in the elementary grades.

> *Grade 3.* Correct use of pronouns, subject-verb agreement, adjectives and adverbs.
>
> *Grade 4.* Be able to recognize a noun, singular and plural nouns, possessive nouns. Pronouns, singular and plural. Verbs, to recognize action and pure [sic] verbs. Recognize adjectives, and classify as descriptive, article, proper, and comparative. Recognize adverbs and use correctly.
>
> *Grade 5.* Recognize common and proper nouns; recognize pronouns; recognize verb phrases.
>
> *Grade 6.* Know the noun as subject and direct object. Know the pronoun as subject and compound subject, and as direct object. Know possessive pronouns. Know the principal parts of irregular and regular verbs. Know the comparison of adverbs. Recognize the preposition and prepositional phrase. Recognize conjunctions and interjections.

The student who follows this program (and it is a state-wide recommendation) is supposed to be able at the end of the sixth grade to name and identify all parts of speech, and to analyze, name, and use the structural elements of the simple sentence. In the following section of this chapter these materials will be found to constitute the textbook content in grammar for grades seven and eight, as well as for grade nine, so that almost total repetition is anticipated.

The program for the elementary schools of the District of Columbia [23] recommends:

Training in language structure will include:
1. Using good sentence structure.
2. Recognition and use of different types of sentences: declarative, interrogative, exclamatory, and imperative.
3. Recognition and use of grammatical terms:
    (*a*) simple subject, (*b*) predicate verb, (*c*) complete subject, (*d*) complete predicate
4. Developing skill in using a verb that agrees in number with the subject.

[23] Public Schools of the District of Columbia, *Language Arts Bulletin* (*Elementary Schools*) (Washington, 1950).

The grammar requirements in grade six of the schools of El Paso, Texas, are described as follows: [24]

> *Topics for Grade 6, Low Group:* subjects and predicates; modifiers of the subject, modifiers of the predicate, phrase modifiers, kinds of sentences, knowledge of parts of speech, common and proper nouns, possessive nouns, nominative pronouns, objective pronouns, possessive pronouns.
> *Topics for Grade 6, High Group:* knowledge of all of the above, plus definition of verbs, all principal parts, tense: past, present, future, adjectives, adverbs, adjective phrases, adverbial phrases, prepositions, connecting words (conjunctions).

Despite a growing movement to postpone the structural and analytical aspects of language instructions to grade seven and beyond, [25] the inspection of courses of study for the language arts in the elementary grades of cities and states will show that a considerable amount of structural and analytical grammar is expected in these grades. The analysis of textbooks of the next section confirms this present fact.

THE EVIDENCE FROM CURRENT TEXTBOOKS

For the materials of this section, five widely used series of language-grammar textbooks were analyzed to determine the number of pages devoted to the teaching of grammar and usage, and the specific items of grammar included in each grade. The series included one for the elementary grades, three for the junior high school grades seven and eight) and two for the senior high school (grades nine to twelve).

(*Junior English in Action,* J. C. Tressler, Marguerite B. Shelmadine, D. C. Heath & Co., New York, 1956, Books 7 and 8.

Better English, Max J. Herzberg, Florence C. Guild, J. N. Hook, Ginn and Co., Boston, 1955, Book 7 and Book 8. Senior High School, Books 9, 10, 11, 12.

[24] El Paso Public Schools, *Tentative Guide for the Language Arts, Grade Six* (El Paso, 1953).
[25] Robert C. Pooley, "Grammar in the Schools of Today," p. 143.

Enjoying English, Don M. Wolfe, Ellen M. Geyer, Lela Tyre Hamilton, L. W. Singer Co., Inc., Syracuse, 1953, Book 7 and Book 8 (Junior High School)

Living Language, Joseph C. Blumenthal, Robert Frank, Louis Zahner, Harcourt, Brace and Co., New York, 1953, Books 9, 10, 11, 12 (Senior High School)

Building Your Language (Grade 3); *Developing Your Language* (Grade 4); *Enriching Your Language* (Grade 5); *Improving Your Language* (Grade 6), Paul McKee, M. Lucile Harrison; Annie McCowan, Houghton Mifflin Co., Boston, 1947)

Grammar in the Elementary Grades

In the single textbook series analyzed for this section, structural grammar, as separated from mechanics and usage, was presented as follows:

Grade 3.   Definition of a sentence
Definitions of *statement* and *question*
Practice in sentence recognition

Grade 4.   Definition of a sentence
Practice in sentence recognition
Definition of a paragraph

Grade 5.   Definition of a sentence
Definition of *noun, verb, adjective, adverb*
Common and proper nouns distinguished

Grade 6.   Definition of a sentence
Kinds of sentences: *declarative, interrogative, imperative, exclamatory*
Subject and predicate
Compound subjects and compound predicates
Definition of a *noun*
Common and proper nouns distinguished
Definition of *singular* and *plural*
Definition of a *verb*
Possessive nouns
Definition of a pronoun
Words in series
Noun of direct address
Appositives
Definition of *adjective* and *adverb*

Definition of *conjunction*
Definition of a *preposition*
Comparison of *adjectives* and *adverbs*
Definition of *positive, comparative, superlative*

The pupils who study this series of books, or one of many similar series, will have been subjected to a considerable portion of the structural grammar of English before reaching the seventh grade. They will have memorized definitions of all the parts of speech; they will be expected to name and identify four kinds of sentences, and to analyze the parts of a simple sentence: subject, predicate, single word modifiers, and phrase modifiers. Nor are the grammatical definitions distinguished by excessive clarity; for example, "A word is used as a preposition when it shows some relation or connection between two other words or ideas." In the sentence *John broke the window,* if a child (sixth grade) said that *broke* is a preposition, who could deny that it clearly shows "some relation or connection" between two other words or ideas?

Grammar in Seventh-Grade Textbooks

Although the textbooks for the elementary grades and many courses of study for grades four through six include grammatical concepts, the seventh-grade books begin with structural grammar as though it were entirely new. For some students, therefore, a portion of the grammatical material is repetition, a repetition which is unhappily to continue through all succeeding grades into college. The topics presented for seventh-grade instruction in the three textbook series for the junior high school (listed as A, B, C) are:

The sentence, definitions, descriptions, A, B, C
Kinds of sentences, A, B, C
Subjects (simple and compound), A, B, C
Predicates, A, B, C
Verbs (simple and compound), A, B, C
Names of all parts of speech, C
Nouns, definition and classes, A, B, C

Verbs, definition and classes, A, B, C
Adjectives, definition, uses, A, B, C
Adverbs, definition, uses, A, B, C
Prepositions, phrases, A, B, C
Agreement of subject and verb, A, B, C
Conjunctions, B
Pronouns, A
Predicate noun and pronoun, A, B, C
Predicate adjective, A, B, C
Pronoun agreement, A
Tense, C
Transitive and intransitive verbs, C
Direct object, A
Compound sentences, A, B, C

Topics added for instruction in the eighth grade:

Tenses and tense forms, A, B
Transitive and intransitive verbs (continued), C
Active and passive voice, B
Natural and inverted order, A
Indirect objects, A, B
Subordination, with conjunctions, B
Participles (gerund) and infinitives, A
Complex sentences, A, B, C
Clauses, treated as adjective, adverb and noun, B

From this analysis it may be observed that the student who follows textbook series A is supposed at the close of the eighth year to know all the parts of speech and all the structural parts of the sentence: simple, compound, and complex sentences, with adjective, adverb, and noun clauses, and all the verbals, participles, gerunds (participle as noun), and infinitives. In series B he will omit the verbals, but must know the active and passive voice of the verb. In series C he will give particular attention to transitive and intransitive verbs, but will omit the verbals.

The teacher of ninth-grade English, receiving students from junior high school classes using these and other texts, and knowing from experience that a very few students know all the grammar that has been taught, and many apparently know none, shrugs his shoulders and starts over again. The ninth-grade texts assume this situation for him, as the analysis below reveals.

Grammar in the Senior High School

Topics presented for instruction in the ninth grade:
    Simple sentence, definition and description
    Subjects
    Verbs
    Nouns
    Pronouns
    Direct objects
    Subjective complements (predicate noun and adjective)
    Adjectives
    Adverbs
    Prepositional phrases
    Compound sentences
    Complex sentences—subordinate clauses
    Verbals
    Appositives

A comparison of this list with that for grades seven and eight reveals no new topic of grammar for the ninth grade other than appositives. The repetition of the entire program of structural concepts is taken for granted. In fact, one of the two senior high school series assumes that the material is entirely new, for section headings are titled, "Meet the adjective," "Now the adverb," "Meet the clause," and so on, in such a manner as to indicate a first acquaintance.

The analysis of the subsequent books for grades ten, eleven, and twelve brings forth no new material in the structure of the sentence, but rather an extensive repetition. The table of contents in grammar for one twelfth-grade book presents these topics for instruction:

    Simple sentence
    Compound sentence
    Complex sentence

Verbals
Agreement of subject and verb
Agreement of pronoun and antecedent

Both teacher and students must feel that they have seen these topics before.

In conclusion, it seems clear from the textbooks here analyzed that the teaching of nearly all the concepts of structural grammar is still performed prior to the end of grade eight, and that no matter how interestingly the grammar may be presented in grades nine through twelve, it is merely the repetition of what has been taught, though generally not learned, in the junior high school. In the extreme case of a student who happened to be subjected to the sequence of textbooks here analyzed, he would have started to define a sentence in the third grade, he would have learned all the parts of speech before the seventh grade, together with the structure of the simple sentence, he would then begin all over again in the seventh grade, but by the eighth grade would have added all or nearly all the concepts of structural grammar. He would then begin anew in the ninth grade, relearning all the concepts of six previous years, and repeating them all over and over through the twelfth grade. If he goes on to college, he frequently turns up with only the haziest notion of the structure of English and begins once again the basic concepts of grammar. In an era devoted to efficiency, this process seems less than perfect.

EVIDENCE FROM THE ESTIMATES
OF EXPERIENCED TEACHERS

To secure an opinion poll of qualified observers, twenty experienced English teachers scattered over the United States were asked to estimate the percentage of teachers who taught grammar from particular points of view. This group included chairmen of departments, present and past supervisors of English in large cities, and present and past officers of the National Council of Teachers of English. All teachers responded to a letter of request, pertinent portions of which are produced below. [26]

By the term *grammar* I mean the structure of English: parts of speech; subject, verb, object, etc.; case, gender, mood, voice, etc.; sentence, phrase, clause; and associated matters of consonance and agreement. I specifically exclude mechanics of writing and problems of usage not related to structure.

To gain, if I may, your impression of the actual situation in the teaching of grammar in the schools under your observation, I am asking your estimate of the percentage of teachers in the area under your observation who indicate, by method of teaching and materials used, one of the three general attitudes toward English grammar described below. I am more concerned with attitudes represented by practice than those expressed in theory. To facilitate your reply I enclose a post card on which you may place your estimates of percentages.

Group I. Traditional grammar. Grammar is essential because it develops the mind. It is the basis for all instruction in English. It must be taught early—in grades 6, 7, and 8, especially—to lay the foundation for future English work. Students must learn rules, identify grammatical elements, analyze sentences. Drill and practice in workbooks or worksheets is the principal method.

Group II. Traditional-functional grammar. Grammar is the means to improved speech and writing. Because it explains usage, grammar must be learned to support usage instruction. Grammar skills are best gained by learning the parts of speech, the elements of the sentence, and the kinds of sentences. These skills may be spread over several years, but are usually all taught before the end of the ninth year. Drill

[26] This letter was addressed to Miriam B Booth, Erie, Pennsylvania; Mrs. Luella B. Cook, Minneapolis, Minnesota; Richard Corbin, Peekskill, New York; Paul Farmer, Atlanta, Georgia; Dorothea Fry, Pasadena, California; Alfred Grommon, Menlo Park, California; Helen Hanlon, Detroit, Michigan; Lucile Hildinger, Wichita, Kansas; J. N. Hook, Champaign, Illinois; Virginia Belle Lowers, Los Angeles, California; Richard Meade, Charlottesville, Virginia; Joseph Mersand, New York, New York; Eula Mohle, Houston, Texas; Helen Olson, Seattle, Washington; John R. Searles, Madison, Wisconsin; Marian Sheridan, New Haven, Connecticut; Blanch Trezevant, Tallahassee, Florida; Fred G. Walcott, Ann Arbor, Michigan; Marian M. Walsh, Louisville, Kentucky; Dorothy Whitted, Delaware, Ohio.

and practice from textbooks and workbooks establishes grammar, which then will function in composition.

Group III. Functional-structural grammar. Grammar is of negligible value in teaching correct usage. Its chief purpose is to develop sentence structure. It should be taught by a plan of slowly developing concepts, a few to each grade from the seventh grade on, constantly inter-related with writing. Grammatical concepts should grow from their use in sentences created by the learner, and not from rules, drills, workbooks or exercises.

Despite the temptation to paint a favorable picture, I hope you will give me your impression of what actually is the typical grammar situation in your schools. My purpose, of course, is to use the evidence you give me to help hasten the improvement we all eagerly desire.

The response may be said to be more than unanimous, inasmuch as all replied and several furnished estimates of two areas, or individual estimates compared to group estimates, the latter by polling groups of teachers.

The table on page 51 presents the distribution of the returns and the averages. Several pertinent observations may be made about these returns. It is obvious, in the first place, that a wide range of opinions exists concerning the point of view from which grammar is taught. The estimates for group I range from 0 to 65 per cent, with an average of 22.2 per cent. Group II estimates are less wide, but they vary from 33 per cent to 94 per cent with an average of 59 per cent. Group III, like Group I, is widely estimated, from 2 per cent to 66 per cent with an average of 18.8 per cent.

In the second place, despite the range of estimates, it seems clear that the point of view represented by Group II description is the prevailing point of view at present in high school grammar teaching.

Third, teachers who rate themselves, as against those who estimate their views, tend to select the Group II description. In city q-2, 94 per cent of the teachers polled placed themselves in Group II; in area s-2, 65 per cent did so likewise.

Percentages of teachers of cities, counties, or geographical areas estimated to hold the attitudes toward structural grammar and described
above by Groups I, II, and III. The entries are arranged by chance and
do not represent the alphabetical order of names in the footnote.

RESPONDENTS	GROUP I	GROUP II	GROUP III
a	50	40	10
b	30	65	5
c-1 (city)	0	50	50
c-2 (rural)	20	75	5
d	50	35	15
e	15	75	10
f	15	75	10
g	65	33	2
h	22	70	8
i	25	65	10
j	1	33	66
k	10	45	40
m	0	55.5	44.4
n	20	70	10
o	20	70	10
p	2	58	40
q-1 (individual)	65	25	10
q-2 (46 teachers) ...	4	94	2
r	10	80	10
s-1 (individual)	30	60	10
s-2 (group)	17	65	18
t	10	50	40
Averages	22.2%	59%	18.8%

It seems fair to draw these conclusions from the table, without
overlooking the informal nature of the inquiry:

1. In the high schools of 1956, in a sampling covering representative centers of the whole United States, the majority of
teachers hold the view that "Grammar is the means to improved
speech and writing. Because it explains usage, grammar must be
learned to support usage instruction. Grammar skills are best
gained by learning the parts of speech, the elements of the sentence, and the kinds of sentences. These skills are usually all taught
before the end of the ninth year. Drill and practice from textbooks
and workbooks establishes grammar, which will then function in
composition."

2. Although the groups are fairly similar in size, there are more teachers at present who hold the traditional, mental discipline point of view (Group I) than there are who believe and practice the concept of slowly developed, cumulative grammar for the purpose of improved sentence structure.

3. Teachers who directly supervise the teaching of others are more optimistic about the numbers of teachers representative of Group III than are heads of departments, professors of English methods, and classroom teachers. (This conclusion is presented without documentation, to avoid identifying particular respondents.)

SUMMARY OF EVIDENCE

The question raised at the beginning of this chapter is, What is the situation in grammar in our schools today? Answers to this question have been sought by studying reports of state-wide English instruction, an analysis of articles in the *English Journal*, the review of some courses of study, the checking of grammar in popular textbooks, and by direct question to leading teachers. The principal answer to the question may be put in the words of Walcott, quoted above (see p. 34): "One is impressed . . . by the extent to which this formal learning and formal drill still dominate the classroom activity, and still supplant the true exercise of self-expression to which they are supposed to contribute." Another answer could be the statement of the present writer in the *English Journal* (see p. 38, footnote): "Grammar as a part of English instruction in elementary and high schools has not changed greatly in the last ten years and shows no sign at the moment of rapid change in the years immediately ahead."

Specifically, the materials of this chapter show that a great number of elementary school children are taught a large number of formal grammatical concepts, that these same materials are begun again in the junior high school and are carried a little farther, and that still the same materials are begun again in the ninth grade of senior high school, and are repeated year after year through the twelfth grade. The results do not in any way justify the time and effort apparently put forth in this endless repetition. Surely there is a better way to teach English and to use grammar effectively in the process. The succeeding chapters of this book outline one possible alternative.

REFERENCES

FARMER, Paul, and FREEMAN, Bernice, *The Teaching of English in Georgia* (Atlanta, Georgia Council of Teachers of English, 1952).

POOLEY, Robert C., "Grammar in the Schools of Today," *English Journal*, Vol. XLIII, No. 3 (March, 1954).

POOLEY, Robert C., and WILLIAMS, Robert D., *The Teaching of English in Wisconsin* (Madison, University of Wisconsin Press, 1948).

WALCOTT, Fred G., "The Limitations of Grammar," *School of Education Bulletin*, University of Michigan, Vol. 19, No. 4 (January, 1948).

VI

New Approaches to Grammar

THE PARTS OF SPEECH

AS HAS BEEN POINTED OUT in the chapter on the development of grammars, study of the parts of speech began with the Greeks. Of the eight parts of speech which we now commonly accept, Aristotle recognized only nouns (in which class he included substantives and adjectives), verbs, and particles (connectives, indeclinable words). As early as the second century before Christ, however, Dionysus Thrax pointed out eight parts of speech: nouns, verbs, participles, articles, pronouns, prepositions, adverbs, and conjunctions—a list much like our own.

The later grammarians had, as we have seen, a decided tendency to copy the work of those who had gone before them. The grammar by Aelius Donatus, written at Rome in the fourth century A.D., lists eight parts of speech only slightly different from those listed by Dionysus Thrax: nouns, pronouns, verbs, adverbs, participles, conjunctions, and interjections. This grammar was a very important one:

Donatus' grammar was much used in later centuries, and the author's name gave to French and to English the word *donat* or *donet*, which, though at first indicating only his own grammar, came to mean any introductory Latin grammar, and finally an elementary treatise on any subject. The employment of this word in English literature of the fourteenth to the sixteenth centuries testifies eloquently to the influence of Donatus upon the study of Latin and of grammar in general during that period. [1]

The system set forth by Donatus is essentially the system used by Lyly in his famous Latin grammar in English and, as we have seen, Lyly's Latin grammar became the model for grammars of English itself. Ben Jonson, for example, followed the Latin grammars in treating both substantives and adjectives as part of the class of nouns, grouping articles and pronouns together, and keeping particles as a separate class. [2]

The terminology used in grammatical studies of Latin and Greek was not, as Jonson's grammar shows, always well suited to the study of English grammar; but this terminology and the concepts it represents still persist. The *N.E.D.* gives illustrations which indicate that since 1509 eight parts of speech have been generally recognized in English, the exception being that sometimes participles, sometimes articles, are as in Latin added to the list and that substantives and adjectives are often grouped together. The end of the eighteenth century saw the more or less definite fixing of the list as we know it. An attempt to eliminate differences in terminology was made by the Joint Committee on Grammatical Nomenclature appointed by the N.E.A., the M.L.A., and the A.P.A., and adopted by these organizations in 1913.

It has often been pointed out that the commonly accepted parts of speech have little to do with the function of words in modern English: "Their use shows at its best in ancient languages . . . where most words bear upon their faces their formal passports, in the shape of inflectional indications which establish automatically to what category they belong." [3] Aiken is one of those who have attempted to modify the formal groupings to meet the demands of the functional change of words in English; Fries is another. It is

[1] Roland G. Kent, *Language and Philology* (Boston, Marshall Jones Co., 1923), p. 130.

[2] *Ibid.*, p. 135.

[3] Janet R. Aiken, *English Past and Present* (New York, Ronald Press, 1930), pp. 242–243.

doubtful, however, that terms which have been in use for so many hundreds of years can easily be replaced.

NOMENCLATURE OF GRAMMAR

Thus, the long history of grammar has brought about very slight variation in the naming of parts of speech and the functions assigned to them. The same conservative influence is to be seen in the general scheme of grammar utilized in describing English. Terminology and the arrangement of elements have remained static over a period of two hundred years in which the organization and nomenclature of almost every other subject of study have changed to a high degree. Only recently has the traditional scheme of grammar been challenged, and while the challenge has been received with respect by professional grammarians, it has not as yet influenced to any observable degree the teaching of grammar in schools and colleges.

Numerous grammarians have made minor alterations in nomenclature to improve what seemed to them to be deficient elements in the traditional system, but they have retained the basic organization. To illustrate: Henry Sweet in *A New English Grammar, Logical and Historical* (1925) accepts the usual classifications as conventionally useful, but coins new terms where he feels the system to be defective. The joining of two or more sentences together he calls a "complex" and adds these definitions: "A complex in which the principal clause is modified by a co-clause is called a co-complex, e.g., 'You shall walk and I shall ride.' " [4] "A complex in which the principal clause is modified by a sub-clause is called a *sub-complex*. . . . A complex which consists of more than two clauses is called an *extended complex*." [5] These and similar variations of nomenclature have almost never been adopted into the commonly taught grammar of the schools.

[4] Henry Sweet, *A New English Grammar, Logical and Historical* (Oxford, Clarendon Press, 1925), p. 162.
[5] *Ibid.*, p. 164.

More extensive recommendations for changes in the traditional system were made by Otto Jespersen in *The Philosophy of Grammar* (1924) and in *Essentials of English Grammar* (1933).

Jespersen states his attitude toward grammar thus:

"Language is . . . a set of habits, of habitual actions. . . . The greater part of these actions are determined by what [the speaker] has done previously in similar situations. . . . But the speaker has to turn these habits to account to meet new situations . . . therefore he cannot be a mere slave to habits, but has to vary them to suit varying needs—and this in course of time may lead . . . to new grammatical forms and usages. Grammar thus becomes a part of linguistic psychology or psychological linguistics. . . ." [6]

Following out his statement that "No linguistic system, however, is either completely rigid or perfectly harmonious, and we shall see . . . that there are loopholes and deficiencies in the English grammatical system," [7] he offers some improvements in definition and terminology. He lists five parts of speech:

(*a*) *substantives*

(*b*) *adjectives*

(*c*) *verbs*

(*d*) *pronouns*, in which he includes *pronominal adverbs* and the articles

(*e*) *particles*, in which he groups adverbs, prepositions, co-ordinating conjunctions, and subordinating conjunctions [8]

To account for the shifts in classification of words as they are used in combinations, he develops the concept of *ranks*. In the phrase *terribly cold weather* the three ranks are exhibited. *Weather*, the substantive is a *primary; cold*, the adjective is a *secondary; terribly*, the adverb, is a *tertiary*. These are the normal correspondences between word class and rank. However, because of the flexibility of English, *primaries* are not only substantives but fre-

---

[6] Otto Jespersen, *The Philosophy of Grammar* (London, G. Allen and Unwin, Ltd., 1935), p. 29.

[7] Otto Jespersen, *Essentials of English Grammar* (New York, Henry Holt and Co., 1933), p. 16.

[8] *Ibid.*, pp. 66–69.

quently adjectives, adverbs, or pronouns. Similarly *secondaries* are not only adjectives, but substantives (a *garden* flower), pronouns, or adverbs. *Tertiaries*, generally adverbs, may also be substantives (come *home*), adjectives, or pronouns. Moreover, a whole phrase may be used as a primary, secondary, or tertiary: *Sunday afternoon* was fine; a *Sunday afternoon* concert; he slept all *Sunday afternoon*.

In addition to the rank terminology, Jespersen employs four other new terms: junction, nexus, adjunct, adnex. *Junction* is the joining of a secondary and a primary so closely "that they may be considered one composite name for what might in many cases just as well have been called by a single name." [9]

> *Examples:* a silly person = a fool
> the warmest season: summer
> a very tall person: a giant

The *adjunct* is the secondary: in the sentences above *silly*, *warmest*, and *tall* are adjuncts. *Nexus* is the joining of a secondary and a primary in such manner that "something new is added to the conception contained in the primary."[10] *Nexus* may be independent, as in *the dress is blue*, or dependent, as in I see *that the door is red*. There is similar dependent nexus in the condensed structures: I painted the door *red;* I hear the dog *bark*. The secondaries in these sentences, *blue, red, bark*, are called *adnexes*.

Without discarding or altering the basic system of English grammar as traditionally taught, Jespersen sought to supply the deficiencies he found in the system. To this end he defined relationships and functions as he found them in the language and created terminology for his new concepts.

REARRANGEMENT OF FAMILIAR TERMS

Janet Rankin Aiken in *A New Plan of English Grammar* (1933) undertakes like Jespersen to improve the traditional system of Eng-

[9] *Ibid.,* p. 91.   [10] *Ibid.,* p. 95.

lish grammar. She begins, "The eight traditional parts of speech, the pillars of the grammatical arch, are seen under logical analysis to be shaky. One, the verb, is a really functional concept. The noun is not one but two functions (subject and complement) while the adjective and adverb together make one (modifier)." [11] She continues to show that prepositions and conjunctions perform one connective function, while the pronoun, traditionally called a part of speech, is really a list of specific words which fulfil any of the six grammatical functions with the exception of the verb. Her system does not abandon the terms *noun, pronoun, adjective,* and *adverb,* but recognizes their logical limitations. The heart of Aiken's system is her analysis of grammar into *unit* and *function.* She calls the main divisions of grammar *Syntax,* the study of word relations, and *Morphology,* the study of word forms.

Syntax has two main divisions: the *syntactical unit,* which is any word or word group performing a syntactical function; and the *syntactical function,* which is the part played by a unit in sentence structure. *Apposition* she classes by itself as a unit which repeats the function of another unit.

The syntactical units are:

a. Sentence (a complete communication in words, containing a verb of independent rank, with its subject)
b. Non-sentence (a complete communication in other than sentence form)
c. Clause (a combination of subject, verb, and complement, or any two of these three)
d. Phrase (two or more words acting together but not constituting a clause)
e. Word (a sound or combination of sounds used to convey a single concept or idea)

Aiken defines syntactical function as the work done by the five syntactical units above. These units perform the following functions:

11 Janet Rankin Aiken, *A New Plan of English Grammar* (New York, Henry Holt and Co., 1933), preface, p. iii.

a. Absolute   (independent)
b. Verb   (dependent)
c. Subject   (dependent)
d. Complement   (dependent)
e. Modifier   (dependent)
f. Connective   (dependent)

Any communication taken as a whole, she says, "is always in the form of a sentence or non-sentence performing an absolute function, and containing one or more units performing one or more of the other five functions. Thus, the absolute is an independent function performed by sentence or non-sentence, while the other five functions operate within the complete unit in a partial or dependent fashion." [12]

In Aiken's system, the exclamation *Not for a million dollars!* would be classified as an independent unit of non-sentence form, while *At the turn of the road he found an old mill which had been abandoned* would be classified as an independent unit (an absolute) in sentence form, containing such units as clauses, phrases, and words, which perform such functions as verb, subject, complement, modifier, and connective.

Another element of terminology in Aiken's system is the use of the word *verbid* to replace *verbal* as the group name for participles, gerunds, and infinitives. She says, "The only useful distinction between verb and verbid is one of idea or intent. The verbid does not convey the sense of completeness expressed by the full verb." [13] This definition is interesting because it places reliance upon the *meaning* of a word as a means of determining its grammatical classification. We shall see below that Fries attempts to discard meaning entirely in the analysis of the grammatical function of a unit of expression.

In summary, then, Aiken presents a well-thought-out arrangement of the traditional elements of English grammar with such new terminology as is necessary to rectify or supply such elements and relationships as she finds defective or lacking in the traditional

[12] *Ibid.*, p. 6.   [13] *Ibid.*, p. 52.

system. In the twenty years since its publication, the sane and reasonable system of Aiken has made no observable impression upon the grammar of English as outlined in the school textbooks.

SOME NEW VIEWS OF ENGLISH GRAMMAR

Fries

A direct challenge to the validity of the traditional scheme of English grammar is made by Fries. [14] Grammar as it is now taught, asserts Fries, is invalid for the true analysis of English. "From the point of view underlying this study, the principles, procedures, the definitions of 'formal grammar' are unsound. . . . Being falsely oriented, 'formal grammar,' as it is studied in relation to English, cannot be expected to provide any satisfactory insight into the mechanisms of our language or any grasp of the processes by which language functions." To proceed from traditional grammar to a scientific analysis of the structure of English, he adds, is no more feasible than to begin chemistry with alchemy or astronomy with astrology.

Utilizing the recorded speech of persons not aware of being recorded, Fries analyzes his data to find answers to such questions as these: What is a sentence? What kinds of sentences are there? What are parts of speech? How do they operate? What are the structural patterns of sentences? What are the "layers" of structure in sentences? The book, as a consequence, is a grammar of the English sentence on entirely new principles, derived exclusively from the observation and analysis of current American English, and organized in terms of a *rationale* derived from the material.

Fries points out that definitions of the English sentence as found in the traditional grammars are based upon meaning (a sentence is a group of words expressing a complete thought) or upon meaning plus grammatical form (a sentence is a meaningful group of

[14] Charles C. Fries, *The Structure of English* (New York, Harcourt, Brace and Co., 1952).

words containing a subject and verb). Such definitions, he avers, do not describe what takes place in practical conversation. His analysis of recorded speech showed that the units of communication were one of these:

1. A single, minimum free utterance.
2. A single free utterance, but expanded, not minimum.
3. A sequence of two or more free utterances.

These observations lead to the author's definition: "We start then with the assumption that a sentence . . . is a single free utterance, minimum or expanded; i.e., that it is 'free' in the sense that it is not included in any larger structure by means of a grammatical device."

All speech consists of communicative utterances or noncommunicative utterances. Of the first type Fries finds three classifications:

  I. Utterances regularly eliciting "oral" responses only:
     A. *Greetings*   B. *Calls*   C. *Questions*
 II. Utterances regularly eliciting "action" responses, sometimes accompanied by one of a limited list of oral responses: *requests* or *commands*.
III. Utterances regularly eliciting conversational signals of attention to continuous discourse: *statements*. [15]

Noncommunicative utterances are those characteristic of situations such as surprise, sudden pain, prolonged pain, disgust, anger, sorrow.

Within an utterance of the communicative type, Fries finds two kinds of meaning: the lexical meaning, which is derived from the dictionary meaning of the words themselves; and the structural meaning, which is the set of signals which indicate such facts as the time of the action, the number of persons or things involved, and their relationship to each other. These devices which signal the structural meanings in an utterance constitute the grammar of a language. It is these devices which we learn unconsciously as we

[15] *Ibid.*, p. 41.

learn our language; without them we could not communicate intelligibly regardless of how many words we knew. "One of the earliest steps in learning to talk is this learning to use automatically the patterns of form and arrangement that constitute the devices to signal structural meaning." [16] Moreover, these devices operate in a system; the items of form and arrangement have signaling significance only as they are parts of patterns in a structural whole. Hence a sentence is a structure made up of form classes or parts of speech.

The structural framework of English, as Fries analyzes it, is made up of four parts of speech and fifteen groups of function words. These constitute the structural signals which convey grammatical meaning in a sentence. The parts of speech are:

Class 1: words which fit into such frames as (The) _____ was good; (the) _____s were good; (the) _____ remembered the _____; (the) _____ went there. In certain positions Class 1 words are used without an article: *Corn is good; he bought bread*

Class 2: words which fit these structural positions:
(The) ___1___ *is/was* _____
_____ *remembered* _____
_____ *went* there

Class 3: In the same frames, words which fit as below:
(The) *good* is/was *good*
The *good* _____s are/were

Class 4: (The) ___3___ ___1___ is/was ___3___ *there*
(The) ___1___ remembered (the) ___1___ *clearly*
(The) _____ went *there rapidly.* [17]

These four parts of speech, Fries concludes, make up the bulk of the "words" in our utterances. It is important to recognize that although many words called "nouns" would fall into class 1, the two categories are not at all identical. In the sentence "The boy went home," *home* would conventionally be classified as a noun, but in Fries's analysis it would be a class 4 word.

---

[16] *Ibid.,* p. 57.   [17] *Ibid.,* pp. 76–86.

In normal communication there is a collection of words fairly small (Fries finds 154 in his recorded materials) which are used with great frequency in English utterances and which are not included in the four parts of speech. These Fries calls "function words" and assorts them into fifteen groups. The first three groups are illustrated here.

Group A: all words for the position in which the word *the* occurs:

A   1   2   3

The concert was good

e.g., *a, an, every, no, my, our, your, some, any, eighteen,* etc.

Group B: words for the position occupied by *may* in this sentence frame:

A   1   B   2   3

The concert *may* be good

e.g., *might, can, could, will, would, should,* etc.

A _____ 1 _____ B _____ 2

The _____ _____ moved

      had, was, got

A _____ 1 _____ B _____ 2

The _____ _____ moving

      was, got, kept

A _____ 1 _____ B

The _____ _____ move

      had to   did

Group C: the word *not* in these constructions:

A   1   B   C   2   3

The concert may *not* be good

A   1   2   C   3

The concert was *not* good

Although the items of these groups are relatively few in number, they are used so frequently as to make up about one-third of the total bulk of the materials studied. [18] These words have also the characteristic of having very little independent lexical meaning, but have rather a meaning closely related to their structural functions.

[18] *Ibid.,* p. 104.

Having classified the words in an utterance, Fries continues with the structural patterns of sentences. Since some utterances result in responses different from those of other utterances, there must be kinds of utterances which can be grouped by identifying characteristics. In classifying these groupings he comments,

the structural signals are in the formal arrangements of the functioning units within the sentence itself. For these, the signals of the kind of sentence are, basically, contrasting arrangements of class 1 and class 2 words. Intonation contrasts are a part of these signals, but they do not often furnish the sole distinguishing feature of the kind of sentence. Certain function words, however, do play an important part in signaling the kinds of utterances we call questions. [19]

From the analysis of the primary elements of the sentence, Fries goes on to the functions performed by words within a sentence. These functions are traditionally described by the terms *subject*, *object*, and *modifier*. These terms, he insists, have no relationship to the actual facts of the real world, but are only names for particular formal structures within an utterance. Hence a *subject* "is simply that class 1 word that is bound to a class 2 word to form the basic arrangement of the sentence and is identified and distinguished from other class 1 words not by meaning but by certain contrastive arrangements." [20] By means of symbols the author demonstrates formulas which account for all the contrastive arrangements of class 1 words. He emphasizes that it is not the meanings of the words themselves but an intricate system of formal features which makes possible the grasp of what we generally call "meaning." "Train boy house take" conveys no meaning; "The boy takes a train to his house" is full of meaning. This meaning is not in the words themselves but in the words as a pattern.

After the analysis of further functions, such as "modifier," Fries describes "Sequence" sentences and "Included" sentences and deals with "Layers of Structure." He is then able to present the ten steps for the analysis of a present-day English sentence. [21] Such analysis can be represented in symbols, e.g.:

[19] *Ibid.*, p. 172.   [20] *Ibid.*, p. 183.   [21] *Ibid.*, pp. 267–268.

D   3   3 1^a f D 1^b 4   2   D   3 1^c f D 1^d f 2 f 1^e
       —   F   —   —   — F   + J   + F   —
       it   it   it   he he   it

In this diagrammatic representation the numbers 1, 2, 3, 4 represent the four parts of speech; D is any "determiner," or Group A form word; f represents a function word, and the capital letter under f, the particular group to which the function word belongs. The letter exponents (1^a, 1^b, etc.) indicate the "referents" of the class 1 words. Words with the same exponent have the same referent. Of this scheme of analysis Fries says, "For this type of analysis it is not necessary to know the lexical meanings of the words nor to know what the sentence is about. One must, however, in determining the structure of class 1 words, either know whether the referent is the "same" or "different," or have another special list of class 2 words." [22]

One of the principal challenges to traditional grammar which Fries makes is with respect to the use of definitions derived from meaning content rather than from form. He asserts, "That the precise lexical meanings of the 'words' are unnecessary [in linguistic analysis] is proved from my use of formulas with symbols to represent whole form classes." [23] As an example he cites the headline "Bus Fares Badly in Emergency," pointing out that with *badly* recognized as a class 4 word, *fares*, in the position it occupies in this utterance, must be a class 2 word. The assumption that the classification may be derived without the aid of lexical meaning seems overconfident. By contrast, note this headline: "Doctor Stoops Low in Medic Meet." Here there can be no assurance of classification until lexical meaning is known. Is *Stoops* a class 2 word? If so, then *Low* is a class 4 word. But if *Stoops* is a class 1 word, then *Low* must be a class 3 word. In such a combination it is impossible to derive the classification exclusively from structural signals. One must know or guess that *Stoops* is a name; i.e., make

[22] *Ibid.*, p. 268.   [23] *Ibid.*, p. 294.

reference to lexical meaning, before he can ascertain accurately the structure.

In the author's example "Bus Fares Badly in Emergency" the classification of *Fares* as a class 2 word rests upon the formal signal *ly* of *Badly*, making it a class 4 word. But compare "Bus Crews Manly in Emergency"; note the *ly* signal which in the formal sense is identical with that of the preceding sentence but in this case *with the aid of lexical meaning only* can be called a class 3 word which in turn identifies *Crews* (also identical in form with *Fares*) as a class 1 word. Structural signals are significant, but apparently cannot be completely divorced from lexical meaning. How would Fries analyze by structural analysis alone the statement, "Professor Rakes Leaves after College Commencement"?

In addition to the doubt cast upon analysis by pure structural means free of lexical meaning, there seems to be a similar difficulty in the function words. In the utterance "The wind blew up the street," *up* is clearly group *F* of the function words (chiefly prepositions). From structure alone "The powder blew up the ship" would seem to demand a similar classification for *up*. How, apart from lexical meaning, can one show the absurdity of this analysis and prove that *up* is a class 3 word? It seems necessary that "meaning" be called upon to clarify structure.

The system of grammar presented by Fries has some very clear advantages. Identifying words in classes according to functional use avoids the "part of speech" problem inherent in the word *mile* in "He walked a mile." Conventional grammar must call *mile* a noun used as an adverb, an awkward explanation. Fries calls it simply a class 4 word. Thus the difficulties of classification arising from functional shift are done away with.

	Fries
I have a *run* in my stocking	Class 1
He can *run* fast	Class 2
The *running* water sparkles	Class 3
The boys came *running*	Class 4

Fries has done a thorough and workmanlike job with his analysis. Convinced that the orientation of traditional grammar is false and that his system provides the means to a scientific analysis of English sentence structure, he has striven to make an objective and systematic description of the organization of English expression in terms which are structural in character. Within the framework of his own goals, he has succeeded admirably.

Whitehall

In his *Structural Essentials of English* [24] Harold Whitehall undertakes to describe the general structural design of English "with a view to clarifying difficulties encountered in the writing of English." Starting from the viewpoint that serious written English is a rather artificial dialect of the current language, Whitehall offers an analysis of its structural detail with attention to the ways this dialect differs from less formal use of English. The principal features of his analysis are:

1. His definition of a word group to avoid the confusions connected with the traditional terms *phrase* and *clause*, and the division of word groups into *headed* and *non-headed*. Headed word groups contain a word identified as the *head* which can be used by itself in all grammatical constructions open to the group. In the word group *five tall trees*, the head word *trees* can stand grammatically wherever the word group can be used. There are four types of headed groups: noun group, verb group, modifier group, and verbal group. *Non-headed* groups can be used in grammatical constructions not open to any single expression within them. No part of the group can substitute for the entire group and make sense. In the subject-verb group *he talks*, neither *he* nor *talks* can substitute for the group; similarly in the prepositional group *of words* neither part can be used for the group. The analysis of the English sentence then rests upon the recognition of the four headed

[24] Harold Whitehall, *Structural Essentials of English* (New York, Harcourt, Brace and Co., 1956).

groups, the two non-headed groups, plus headed groups of more than one head (*he and I, John and Henry*).

2. The relationship of rhythm to pattern in English by the factors of relative voice loudness or *stress*, relative voice frequency or *tone*, and interruption of the normal movement from one speech sound to the next, or *juncture*. "Every normal speaker of English signals the grammatical structure of his statements by the use of *tone*, *stress*, and what is nowadays called *juncture*." [25] In written English it follows that the writer must be able to present the grammatical signals that a speaker might use so that they are understandable to a reader.

3. The analysis of sentence patterns into three classes of "sentence situations." Sentence situation I consists of subject and verb or verb group predicate; situation II is subject-verb-complement; situation III contains two complements, an *inner complement* and an *outer complement* added to subject and verb (example: The boys gave their sister (inner complement) a doll (outer complement). These patterns show the fixed word order which is characteristic of the English subject-verb sentence and may be summarized thus: "In the subject-predicate sentence, the subject, the verb, any inner complement, and any outer complement occur in a fixed 1, 2, 3, 4 order." [26]

4. His analysis of "word forms" (the surviving inflectional forms of English words) into three major functional approaches. Approach I is the study of the shapes of words (see, sees, saw; who, whom, etc.). Approach II is called *substitution* and is the use of words or word groups as substitutes for preceding or following elements in a context (as, for example, the use of an appropriate pronoun in relation to a preceding noun). Approach III is called selection: it is the grammatical device by which one word or construction can dictate the choice of form in another (example: *John* is strong; *he* can lift *his* bicycle with *his* left hand). Selection affects number, gender, person, and case in the choice of forms.

[25] *Ibid.*, p. 20.　　　　　　　　[26] *Ibid.*, p. 40.

These few items may serve to illustrate the use of structual linguistics which Whitehall employs in his analysis of the grammar of English and the freshness of approach which results. His analysis constantly rewards the reader with new insights into grammatical relationships not previously realized or at least not so clearly seen. By a happy blend of the resources of current linguistics with his own originality of analysis, he offers a most interesting, readable, and challenging approach to the study of English grammar.

Roberts

Of particular interest to high school teachers is Paul Roberts' *Patterns of English.* [27] In this book he attempts a bridge over that gap which exists between the work of the structural linguists and the traditionally trained high school teacher of English. He claims, with justice, to be the first to make a structural analysis of English for high school use. He says in his introduction,

I have no intention here of attacking or ridiculing the older ways of presenting the English language in the schools. . . . When I came in touch with linguistic science, I reacted against it and wished to defend the tradition. But when I tried to, I found the tradition largely indefensible. I found myself giving ground . . . until I was forced to the realization that the picture of the language I was giving my students was false . . . falsely grounded. [28]

In his analysis of the structure of English, Roberts reflects the influence of Fries, particularly in his use of four basic "form classes" and a cluster of "structure groups" which he classifies into three divisions: the determiners, the auxiliaries, and the intensifiers. So far as is possible Roberts uses the familiar grammatical nomenclature, though with specific restrictions to overcome the ambiguities of traditional definitions. Hence his four form classes are designated nouns, verbs, adjectives, and adverbs. These form classes are, of course, very large, containing thousands of words. In contrast

[27] Paul Roberts, *Patterns of English* (New York, Harcourt, Brace and Co., 1956).

[28] *Ibid.,* introduction, pp. 1, 2.

the structure groups are small, some groups containing only a word or two. Nevertheless, it is the structure words which make the sentence "go"; this fact may be demonstrated in nonsense poems in which the form class words may all be novel, but the structure words must present a known pattern for the verse to hang together.

Roberts defines his form classes in terms of pattern: "a verb is a word that patterns like *sing*, *beautify*, or *arrive*. That is, it is a word which occurs in positions like those in which *sing*, *beautify*, and *arrive* occur." [29] His analysis of English grammar is the demonstration of the way in which form classes and structure words combine to create the patterns of English expression.

Especially interesting is the development of intonation and punctuation in Part Eight of the book. Here, like Whitehall, he analyzes the part that *stress*, *pitch*, and *juncture* play in our use of language, and the relationship between these elements af speech and their corresponding signals in written English. He points out that punctuation is often regularized by editors, and that it is well to let word structure guide the writer to punctuation wherever it will. But in those situations where word structure is not a good guide, knowledge of intonation patterns will help. After all, he points out that punctuation arose as a response to original speech intonations.

Patterns of English is a challenging invitation to the task of rewriting the grammar of English for use in secondary schools. In his sensible and reasonable approach to the undertaking, Roberts will undoubtedly stand as a leader and pioneer in directing the work of all who will labor in the task of fitting the research of linguistic scholars to the needs of classroom English teachers.

CONCLUSIONS

How soon will the grammar of the schools reflect the new approaches to grammar as set forth in this chapter; particularly the

[29] *Ibid.*, p. 13.

schemes of Fries, Whitehall, Roberts, and those who will follow? The evidence from society and education in general is that the complete accomplishment of such a change will be slow. Generations of teachers must be trained in the new understandings and techniques; current school books will have to be abandoned or rewritten, and tests and other evaluative devices will have to be altered or replaced. Such things take time. The lag of inertia will be great. Nevertheless, there is without question an awakening of interest in structural linguistics and its applications to the teaching of English. Here and there at the present time are a few forward-looking and experimental teachers using the materials now available. They will create disciples. It is interesting to recall that the first half of the twentieth century has witnessed a notable change of attitude and teaching technique in the field of English usage. It seems probable that the second half of the century will witness the revolution in English grammar and its teaching which appears inevitable.

The question may well be asked, Where does this book fit into the changing pattern of grammar teaching? The point of view is obviously sympathetic to the work of the structural linguists, yet the grammar is presented in traditional patterns. Two answers may be offered. First, the change in grammatical terminology and technique will occupy much time. There are countless numbers of young people now in the schools who can be saved needless repetition and aimless teaching while following the traditional patterns of English grammar. There are thousands of teachers traditionally trained who are willing to teach grammar intelligently and effectively if given a plan and a purpose. Such teachers will hasten the movement from the traditional system to one more nearly approaching the linguistic viewpoint if given a workable transition. Second, and this is a major consideration, the structural linguists thus far have been primarily interested in analysis. For descriptive purposes, analysis is basic. But the English teacher in school or college is concerned with synthesis in language, that is, writing.

He needs analysis for the purpose of understanding the language he is teaching, but for the improvement of writing he requires a system which emphasizes the manner in which the elements of structure combine to produce better sentences; to create clear, meaningful, and interesting prose. To emphasize structure to these ends is the purpose of this book.

REFERENCES

AIKEN, Janet Rankin, *A New Plan of English Grammar* (New York, Henry Holt and Co., 1933).

AIKEN, Janet Rankin, *English Past and Present* (New York, The Ronald Press, 1930).

FRIES, Charles C., *The Structure of English* (New York, Harcourt Brace and Co., 1952).

JESPERSEN, Otto, *Essentials of English Grammar* (New York, Henry Holt and Co., 1933).

JESPERSEN, Otto, *The Philosophy of Grammar* (London, G. Allen and Unwin, Ltd., 1924).

KENT, Roland G., *Language and Philology* (Boston, Marshall Jones Co., 1923).

ROBERTS, Paul, *Patterns of English* (New York, Harcourt Brace and Co., 1956).

SWEET, Henry, *A New English Grammar, Logical and Historical* (Oxford, Clarendon Press, 1925).

WHITEHALL, Harold, *Structural Essentials of English* (New York, Harcourt Brace and Co., 1956).

VII

The Background of Surviving Inflections

TO ANYONE WHO HAS STUDIED a modern foreign language such as French, German, or Spanish the relative simplicity of English grammatical structure is at once apparent. This fact does not make English an easy language for a foreigner to learn; on the contrary, because meaning now depends so much upon word order and idiomatic construction, English is really harder to learn than if our grammar were more highly inflected. English once had a grammar involving a large number of inflected forms. In the course of its development in the last fifteen hundred years, English has gradually lost most of its earlier inflections. As the inflections went, the meanings which they formerly indicated were expressed by words used in combination, like prepositional phrases, or by the order in which words were placed in an utterance. Thus, as our language shed more and more of its grammatical inflections, word order and phrasal groups became increasingly important. This chapter will discuss the surviving inflections in modern English, with a glimpse at their sources. This aspect of language is technically called *accidence* or *morphology*, the study of forms. The next chapter will deal with patterns of words and word order, a study technically named *syntax*. In modern English, meaning is conveyed both by morphology (as in *sing, sang, sung*) and by syntax (as in *Father spanked the baby*). Most English sentences contain some remnants of inflected forms, as are found in pronouns, the *s* on the plural of nouns, and the various parts of the verb *to be*. But for clarity of understanding we tend to rely more upon the order in which the words are placed than upon their differing grammatical forms. We have very little difficulty understanding an uninflected statement such as *John take stone break window* provided the words are arranged in the expected order. Yet the same words out of order, but with full inflection, would confuse us: *Windows stones takes breaks John*. In the following sections the various parts of speech in modern English will be taken up in turn with enough background of earlier inflections to explain the forms which still survive.

THE NOUN

In Old English there were two basic patterns for the declension of nouns, the strong declension (characterized by stems ending in vowels, such as *a, o, u*) and the weak declension (characterized by stems ending in the consonant *n*); the strong declension had further variations of its own, two of which are exhibited here for the words *stone* and *son*.

	Singular	*Plural*	*Singular*	*Plural*
Nominative	stan	stanas	sunu	suna
Genitive	stanes	stana	suna	suna
Dative	stane	stanum	suna	sunum
Accusative	stan	stanas	sunu	suna

By means of these inflected forms, certain ideas were expressed concerning the noun which today are expressed by a phrase or by a survival of the earlier inflected form. The nominative case indicated the subject of a statement; the genitive case, possession; the dative case, the direction of an action as now expressed by *to* or *for;* and the accusative case indicated the object of an action. Of these inflections we have surviving in regular use only the -*s* from the nominative plural which we attach to nearly all nouns today to indicate a plural, and the -*s* of the singular genitive by which we express possession with most nouns. The possessive plural can rarely be detected in speech (we say *The Smiths' house* or *the*

Joneses' house). In writing we indicate the possessive by the addition of an apostrophe after the *-s* of the plural. These are purely formal distinctions in writing and are not essential to meaning, as can be demonstrated by their absence in speech.

From the strong noun forms we derive chiefly the *-s* sign of the genitive and of the plural. From the weak declension in Old English, which had *-n* or *-en* as its chief characteristic, we get such plurals as *oxen* and *children*, and the poetic *kine* (plural of cow). Some Old English nouns indicated a plural by a change of vowel. From certain phonetic causes in the previous history of these words, the vowel of the singular form becomes changed in the plural to a sound more forward in the mouth. By this process, technically called *umlaut*, we derive such pairs as *mouse, mice; louse, lice; goose, geese*. In the development of English some nouns made no distinction between the singular form and the plural form. Chaucer says of his Knight "his hors weren goode," in which phrase the plural verb *weren* indicates that *hors* is a plural. Today we use *sheep* for singular and plural and often *fish* the same way. Of these two, *sheep* as a plural is a historical form like *hors* above, whereas *fish* as a plural is a specialized use of the singular form. A similar use is customary with *pound* and *dozen*.

THE PRONOUN

Old English had complete or partial declensions for the personal, interrogative, and demonstrative pronouns. The personal pronoun declension included, in addition to the forms shown here, forms for the dual number (two persons) in the first and second persons.

FIRST PERSON

	SING.	PLU.
Nom.	ic	wē
Gen.	mīn	ūser, ūre
Dat.	mē	ūs
Acc.	mec, mē	ūsic, ūs

SECOND PERSON

	SING.	PLU.
Nom.	þū	gē
Gen.	þīn	ēower, īower
Dat.	þē	ēow, īow
Acc.	þec, þē	ēowic, ēow, īow

THIRD PERSON

		SING.		PLU.
	Masc.	*Fem.*	*Neuter*	*(All genders)*
Nom.	hē	hēo	hit	hīe
Gen.	his	hiere	his	hiera
Dat.	him	hiere	him	him
Acc.	hine	hīe	hit	hīe

Modern English still uses most of the inflected forms to indicate pronoun function, but with certain modifications in the number of cases and in form. We do not distinguish dative and objective cases but use one form, usually that of the old dative. This form shows both the direction and the object of an action. The change to a combined "objective" case had begun in Old English, as is seen from the fact that accusative forms identical with the dative forms were already being used. The merger of the two cases was completed by the start of the Middle English period. Today we have only two distinct second person forms, *you,* and *your* or *yours.* They are taken from the Old English plural forms. Around the thirteenth century, English used the singular forms *thou, thine,* and *thee* only for familiar address to servants, children, and social inferiors, and began to employ the plural forms for polite address, even to one person. By the sixteenth century the polite (plural) form was extended to general use in the singular. Gradually the original singular forms went out of use except by the Quakers. *Ye,* the nominative, and *you,* the objective, became confused in ordinary usage, and eventually *you* was used for both functions. (In the same way, the Quakers came to use *thee* for both nominative and objective.) In the third person feminine and neuter singular, the initial sound changed. English had become a language which used natural gender, and that fact may have encouraged the adoption of forms which made the pronouns for the genders distinct from one another. As late as the sixteenth century, *it* was still the genitive form, but was gradually replaced by *its*. This change brought the form in line with the other noun and pronoun genitives. Our modern initial *th* in the third person plural forms resulted from Scandinavian borrowing after the eighth century. These Scandinavian forms gradually spread southward throughout England and became the accepted forms. Because some second and third person forms are identical, we have to depend on sentence structure to determine number and function when they are used. We can still say, however, that we do have an active system of personal pronoun inflections.

We also have a set of inflected forms for the interrogative pronouns. Here too the number of cases has been reduced to three: nominative, genitive, and objective. Old English had one interrogative pronoun, *hwa*. From its masculine nominative, genitive, and dative forms, *hwa, hwaes, hwaem*, we get the modern *who, whose, whom*. From the neuter nominative and accusative form, *hwaet*, we take *what*. *Hwi*, the instrumental case (the case of the agent of action) gives us *why*.

For the demonstrative pronouns, Old English had a full system of inflections in all genders. There were two pronouns, *that* (using the same forms as the definitive article) and *this*. We have lost almost all the inflectional forms. We have kept only a singular and plural form for each word: *that, those; this, these*. The forms come from the neuter nominative singular and the nominative plural of each word, with some sound shifts in the plurals. Our other modern pronoun classes such as reflexive and relative were not used in Old English, and the indefinite pronouns were not inflected. Despite some simplifications a large number of the pronoun inflections have survived into modern English. This has come about because pronouns are used so frequently and because they show relationships that would be hard to express without the use of distinctly different forms.

THE ADJECTIVE

Old English adjectives had two declensions, strong and weak, for all the cases. When the adjective was used with a noun that did not have a definite article or similar word (such as a demonstrative or possessive pronoun), the strong declension was used. If the noun had a definite article or similar word, the weak declension was used. *Good man* shows the adjective in the strong position. Its Old English form was *god mann*. In the weak position, as in *the good man*, the Old English form was *se goda mann*. By the Middle English period almost all these adjective forms had been lost. Each declension had kept only one singular and one plural form. In the weak declension the surviving forms were alike. Before the end of the Middle English period, the strong forms were also the same. Thus, modern English inherited only one form for each adjective. Today we make no distinction for case, number, or gender.

The modern adjective does change to show degrees of comparison. The endings used for regularly compared adjectives are about the same as they were in Old English. Old English used *-ra* for the comparative, and *-est* or *-ost* for the superlative. These have become our modern *-er* and *-est*. Thus, Old English *heard, heardra, heardost* become modern English *hard, harder, hardest*. Old English also had irregular comparisons, in which the comparative and superlative forms came from roots which were different from the positive. Modern English still uses most of them. For example, *good, better, best* was *god, betra, betst* in Old English. In addition, a few Old English adjectives formed the superlative with the ending *-umo*. By analogy these were also given the *-est* ending, producing a "new" ending, *-most*. From this source we get such modern superlatives as *hindmost* and *inmost*.

The modern English article, like the attributive adjective, has no surviving inflections. In Old English, the article had a full set of inflections, but all that survive are the forms that have become relative and demonstrative pronouns.

It is easy to see that modern English gets along well without the complicated system of adjective inflections which it has lost. We can tell what we need to know from the noun which the adjective modifies. Thus, only one form is needed for each adjective.

THE VERB

The modern English verb inflections are much less complicated than those of Old English. Like Old English, English today has two main sorts of verbs. The first is the regular or weak verb, such as *walk*. The principal parts of a weak verb are based on the form of the infinitive. The past tense and past participle are formed by adding the ending *-ed*, giving *walk, walked, walked*. The present participle is formed by adding *-ing, walking*. The second kind of verb is the irregular or strong verb, such as *sing*. The principal parts of a strong verb are formed by means of changes of the chief vowel instead of with endings. Thus, the principal parts of *sing* are *sing, sang, sung*. Not all strong verbs have the same vowel changes. The changes depend mainly upon what class of Old English verb the modern verb comes from.

There were seven distinct classes of Old English strong verbs, grouped according to the pattern of the vowel changes. The vowel changes in one particular class are responsible for one modern problem. Although the past of *sing* is *sang*, the past of *cling* is not *clang*, but *clung*. This inconsistency can be explained. Old English strong verbs had two past forms, singular and plural. The singular form ordinarily survived. In the particular class mentioned, namely, the third class, it happens that both the past plural form and the past participle had the same vowel, *u*. For some reason, the plural past form survived in part of the verbs of this class. As a result, analogy can cause the learner to form the principal parts of a less familiar verb of this class incorrectly. He cannot apply the *ring, rang, rung* vowel sequence to such a verb as *sting*.

Besides the weak and strong verbs, there are a few called anomalous verbs. Even in Old English these verbs were unusually irregular in forming their principal parts. They include such verbs as *do, did, done; go, went, gone;* and *be, was, been.* The variation in the forms of the anomalous verbs usually results from the combination of two or more prehistoric verbs. The forms of three prehistoric verbs are used in the conjugation of *be.* The anomalous verbs are ones which we use very frequently. That probably explains why they have never become more like other verbs.

Fortunately, most English verbs are now weak. English began to lose strong verbs in the early Middle English period. Some dropped out of the language entirely because they were no longer used, or because they were replaced by foreign weak verbs. At the same time, many strong verbs were made into weak verbs by adding the regular weak endings to the strong infinitive form. Only a few new strong verbs came into the language. The added ones were from foreign sources, or resulted from analogy with existing strong verbs. By analogy with such verbs as *weave, wove, woven,* we get the alternate strong past participle form *proven* instead of *proved.* As a result of the tendency to lose strong verbs, we have today fewer than one hundred strong verbs in English. This number is not likely to increase because new verbs are almost always in the weak pattern. Even in the weak verbs themselves, modern English shows greater simplicity. Old English had three kinds of weak verbs, depending on the differences in prehistoric forms. Two of the three types had somewhat different conjugations, while the third type was becoming assimilated with the first two. Today we consider all weak verbs in a single class. Thus, by reducing the number of verb types, modern English has made a great gain in simplicity. It has made further simplifications by reducing the over-all number of strong verbs and increasing the number of weak verbs. Learning the principal parts of the more irregular of the existing verbs is relatively easy because these verbs are used so frequently.

The modern English verb can be called complex in one respect. It has been given six tenses, whereas the Old English verb had only two: present and past. What we call the compound tenses (perfect tenses and future) were just beginning to develop in Old English. The earliest examples occur in material which had been translated verbatim from Latin, which had compound tenses. The added tenses of modern English do not actually add new forms. They make use of the existing forms of the verb, compounded with *have* and *shall* and *will*. We can illustrate by comparing the tense possibilities in Old English and modern English, using the verb *sing* (Old English *singan*):

OLD ENGLISH	(tense)	MODERN ENGLISH
ic singe	present	I sing
	pres. perfect	I have sung
ic sang	past	I sang
	past perfect	I had sung
	future	I shall sing
	fut. perfect	I shall have sung

We see that the four additional tense ideas are expressed by combinations. The perfect tenses use the past participle, and the future uses the present form. Old English did have some method of showing further gradations in time by using other elements within the sentence. For example, adverbs of time could be used to give a future meaning to a present verb. We still use this method today. We say, "I *will take* the first train tomorrow," or "I *am taking* the first train *tomorrow*," or "I *take* the first train *tomorrow*." Although only the first version uses the future tense of the verb, the future idea is made clear in the other two versions by the adverb *tomorrow*. By such word use, Old English was able to supplement its two-tense system. With the addition of four tense forms, modern English can present differences in time relationships more clearly and economically.

Besides adding considerably to the tense system without adding new forms, modern English has reduced the number of separate forms in the present and past tenses. A comparison of the Old English and modern English conjugations of the weak verb *cemban* (modern English *comb*) shows this change.

Present tense		Past tense	
Old Eng.	Mod. Eng.	Old Eng.	Mod. Eng.
cembe (1)	comb ⎫ (1)	cembde (1)	combed ⎫
cembst (2)	comb ⎬	cembdest (2)	combed ⎪
cembð (3)	combs (2)	cembde	combed ⎬ (1)
cembaþ ⎫	comb	cembdon ⎫	combed ⎪
cembaþ ⎬ (4)	comb	cembdon ⎬ (3)	combed ⎪
cembaþ ⎭	comb	cembdon ⎭	combed ⎭
(4 forms)	(2 forms)	(3 forms)	(1 form)

In the present tense, Old English required three separate forms in the singular plus a plural form. Modern English uses one form for all persons except third singular, where -*s* is added. (Certain verbs such as *ought, must,* and *can* are exceptions. Their third person forms come from old past tense forms. Also, the third person -*eth* ending still survives in some Bible translations as in "He restoreth my soul.") In the past tense, Old English used three separate forms. Modern English has only one form. We recall that in the compound tenses a single combination of forms serves for singular and plural in all persons. Therefore, the modern weak verb requires only four distinct forms for all uses: third person present form, regular present form (used also in future tense), present participle, and past form (used also in perfect tenses). Those modern strong verbs which have separate past and past participle forms require five forms. Thus *walk,* a weak verb, requires four forms: *walk, walks, walking,* and *walked. Sing,* a strong verb with separate past and past participle takes five forms: *sing, sings, singing, sang,* and *sung.* Because of its special origin, *be* has eight forms: *am, are, is, was, were, be, being,* and *been.* We are not usually conscious that *be* has so many forms. We use them so often that remembering them is not a problem. With the exception of the few verbs like *be*, modern English has achieved considerable economy in the number of present and past forms.

Modern English has also added some variations within the tenses. We make considerable use of the emphatic and the progressive. This gives a greater variety of expression than many other languages have. For example, in German one says *ich singe*. In English one may say *I sing, I do sing* (emphatic), or *I am singing* (progressive). All express a present idea, but each gives a different shade of meaning. The emphatic form uses the verb *do*, and the progressive uses *be* plus the present participle. This added flexibility of expression is a further advantage of modern English.

Modern English has lost many of the mood distinctions of Old English. We depend mainly on the indicative. The imperative no longer has separate forms of its own. We recognize the imperative by other means since its forms are the same as those of the indicative. Frequently the subject is omitted ("Leave the room at once.") or an exclamation point is used ("You leave this room at once!"). In spoken language we depend on tone of voice. The subjunctive mood retains some forms of its own, but is not used very much any more. We do use the subjunctive for conditional statements such as, "If I were ready, I would leave now." We also retain some stock subjunctive expressions, such as "Long live the queen."

We can readily see that the verb has lost a great part of the complex inflection system it had in Old English. The majority of the verbs are now weak. The remaining strong verbs are mostly ones which are commonly used and therefore less troublesome to learn. The number of separate forms used has been reduced by about half. At the same time, the verb has taken on additional ability to make distinctions. The four added tenses make it possible to show time relationships clearly. The use of the emphatic and progressive forms also adds flexibility. The result is that the modern English verb is able to convey gradations of meaning beyond the ability of Old English with a simpler system of inflections.

THE ADVERB

Most modern English adverbs fall into one of two groups, flat (no ending) or with the standard ending of -*ly*. This difference in adverbs can be traced to the types of adjectives from which adverbs were formed in Old English. The customary way to form an adverb from an adjective was to add the suffix -*e*. Thus the adjective *heard* (modern *hard*) became the adverb *hearde* (modern *hard* meaning *vigorously*). Eventual dropping of the final *e* produced an adverb identical in form to the adjective from which it came. *Hard, slow,* and *fast* are examples of flat adverbs. Adverbs with the standard ending -*ly* are more usual in modern English. These adverbs have a more complicated history. They are based on adjectives which were themselves formed from nouns. In forming such an adjective the suffix -*lic* was added. In this way the noun *freond* (modern *friend*) was the basis for the adjective *freondlic* (modern *friendly*, literally *friendlike*). This adjective was then made into an adverb by the addition of the adverbial suffix -*e*, giving *freondlice* (*in a friendly manne*r). Later the combined ending -*lice* was thought of as an adverbial ending. It was then added directly to adjectives. Thus the adjective *eornost* (modern *earnest*) became the adverb *eornostlice* (*earnestly*). (According to the regular rule it would have become *eorneste* (modern *earnest*.) This later ending -*lice* became shortend to -*ly*, the form most generally used for modern adverb formation. As a result, the flat adverb is much less common and there is sometimes a tendency to add -*ly* to legitimate flat adverbs. Both *slow* and *slowly* are accepted as adverbs in good usage. An additional problem is the fact that a number of modern adjectives also maintain the -*ly* ending, such as *kindly, friendly,* and *lowly*.

There are a few modern adverbs which have unusual forms and come from other sources. A few come from Old English genitive singular noun forms, which had the ending -*es*. This ending came to have adverbial status and accounts for such modern adverbs as *days, nights,* and *needs,* as used in, "He must needs work nights and sleep days." There are also adverbs which are not based upon other words but which came into use for particularly adverbial concepts. This group includes such common words as *here, there,* and *up.*

Although the adverb shows the results of inflection in its forms, it is no longer actively inflected except to show degrees of comparison. This is usually done by means of the words *more* and *most.* Flat adverbs, however, are also compared by means of the suffixes *-er* and *-est.* These endings are used in comparing adverbs ending in *-ly* if the resultant word is acceptable to the ear, as in *early, earlier, earliest.* For many adverbs of two syllables and all adverbs of three or more syllables, comparisons are expressed by *more* and *most.*

REFERENCES

Bryant, Margaret, *Modern English and Its Heritage* (New York, The Macmillan Co., 1948).

Moore, Samuel, and Knott, Thomas A., *The Elements of Old English* (Ann Arbor, Mich., George Wahr, 1934).

Robertson, Stuart, and Cassidy, Frederic G., *The Development of Modern English,* 2nd ed. (New York, Prentice-Hall, Inc., 1954).

Wright, Joseph, and Wright, Elizabeth Mary, *Old English Grammar* (New York, Oxford University Press, 1914).

VIII

English Sentence Patterns

REFERENCE WAS MADE in the previous chapter to the growing significance of word order in English communication because of the gradual loss of inflectional forms. In nouns the nominative and accusative cases, once clearly distinguished from other cases by inflectional endings, now are distinguished only by position in the word order of the sentence. In *John likes candy*, no one accustomed to English would misunderstand that the subject of the verb is *John* in the nominative case, and that the object of the verb is *candy* in the accusative or objective case. If the two nouns are reversed, *Candy likes John*, an English speaker recognizes at once that *Candy* must be the name of a person or animal since it is the subject, and that the object of the verb is now *John*. This plan or pattern of word order is a signal of meaning so significant that it governs a large portion of the structure of English statements, and deviations from it, as we shall see below, indicate a purpose other than a statement, or else indicate unusual emphasis.

So strong in our minds is this pattern of subject-verb-object (hereafter referred to as S-V-O) that it affects constructions in popular speech and writing to which it does not historically apply. The history and logic of grammar would call for *This is I* in a statement of identity. But the strong force of pattern, expecting an objective case after a verb in a simple three-part pattern induces the ungrammatical *This is me* to the point that it has become tolerated, if not fully approved, and creates the less acceptable but

87

very common constructions *This is him, this is her.* Similarly an old dative case has been transformed into a nominative case by the force of pattern in the statement "(To) me was given the responsibility." The dative *to me* was once indicated by a pronoun form. As this form merged with the accusative, the initial *me* was felt to be ungrammatical in standing before a verb in the position of a subject, and so was changed by common speech to *I.* Therefore we have the peculiar construction in modern English of a passive verb, which is not supposed to have an object, apparently forced to have one. The old subject, *responsibility*, which followed the verb, is now called "a retained object" because the old dative *to me* has become a subject, *I.*

These illustrations serve to show that word order forming sentence patterns is a powerful factor in the grammar of modern English.

It would almost seem that English expression would be forced into rigid molds which might render meaning clear, but would be dull and monotonous by reason of repetition. Fortunately English has the resources to retain the values of a fairly fixed word order and at the same time create enough variety to lend interest and sparkle to the expression of ideas. The thesis of this book is that the teaching of grammar in schools has this very purpose as its foundation: *to show how the materials of English sentences are assembled to create a happy blend of clear meaning and interesting variety of structure.*

THE BASIC PATTERN

The formula underlying the structure of English sentences is S-V-O, standing for subject, verb, object. The following illustrations show how this formula governs structure in sentences of increasing complexity:

John loves Mary.
Five boys took apples from the barrel.

A boy and a dog chased the frightened rabbit.
To drive a hard bargain gave him pleasure.
Climbing the steep slope forced John to pant.
How he would get his mired vehicle out of the mud perplexed the
exasperated driver.

These sentences show not only the regularity of the formula,
but a few samples of the almost infinite variety of detail to be patterned under the general scheme of S-V-O.

Other sentence patterns use a modification of the formula. The
sentence using a verb of identity or relationship (sometimes called
a copulative verb) does not have an object since the verb expresses
no action, but does have a complement which regularly follows the
verb. Here are examples:

John was angry.
Mary seemed bored.
The lawyer became chairman.
The rescued sailors looked exhausted.

Another similar pattern employs an intransitive verb, or a verb
whose action governs the agent performing the action. Such verbs
do not take objects, but the pattern of S-V applies, as follows:

Tom panted.
The train raced for five miles.
Five teams rowed across the lake.

The pattern of command, called the imperative sentence, employs the basic pattern with the subject generally implied rather
than expressed. The pattern might be expressed (S)-V-O, as in:

Shut that door!
Take off your hat!
Please put all empty cartons into the trash barrel.

Sometimes to secure the attention of a particular person or group
the subject is named, in which case the full S-V-O pattern generally applies:

You, there, pick up those papers!
All passengers go to boat stations and put on life-jackets!

VARIATIONS FROM THE BASIC PATTERN

Despite the regularity of pattern in English sentences, variations from the basic pattern do occur in most continuous passages of prose and are even more frequent in verse. Changes in the basic pattern of S-V-O are usually called *inversions*. Two simple inversions are:

1. Verb before subject:
   Came then the expected blow.
   Mightily roared the guns from Shiloh Ridge.
2. Object before subject and verb:
   Great courage he showed in this effort.
   Full command the admiral assumed after the death of his superior. [1]

These inversions have the effect of emphasizing the idea put first and are employed for purposes of emphasis and variety. They are used cautiously and infrequently by good writers, who realize how easily this type of emphasis can become wearisome or absurd. Nevertheless, they are available for effective use where appropriate.

A more conventional inversion is created by the use of words call *expletives*, such as *it* and *there*. Their use permits the inversion of subject and verb without the excessive emphasis felt when the verb begins a sentence. Compare:

Were five people present. (statement)
There were five people present.
Five people were present.

The first sentence suggests the word order of a question, to be discussed below. The second is a very common sentence type permitting an almost unnoticed inversion. The third is the basic pattern and is more likely to be used where stress is desired on the adjective, in this case the number *five*. Other examples of inversion by means of an expletive are:

[1] These inversions seem unnatural out of context.

It never rains here in September.
It took him a long time to find his ticket.
There comes a time for everything.
There followed a long discussion of ways and means.

The first example is a fixed pattern or idiom of English. Events of weather are generally expressed with the expletive *it* followed by a verb: it snows, it blows, it's hot, it's cold, it's cloudy, and so on. The other three examples show a pattern of great frequency in which the use of the expletive permits the postponement of the subject. This type of inversion provides a pleasant variation from the S-V-O pattern in running prose.

Asking a question in English is accomplished in speech by (*a*) an inverted word order; (*b*) a rising voice intonation; or (*c*) a combination of the two:

a. Were the boys at the station (?) (may be queried without voice rise)
b. The boys were already at the station   (?) (with voice rise)
c. Were the boys already at the station (?) (voice rise and inversion)

In written English a question is indicated by the use of a sign at the end of the question, the familiar question mark (?). This mark is employed whether or not the interrogative nature of the words is indicated by an inverted order.

You took the wrong bus?
Did you take the wrong bus?

The second illustration shows a formula for questions in English. If the verb to be used has an auxiliary, this auxiliary is placed before the verb in the question pattern.

Statement: He has a fine voice.
Question: Has he a fine voice?

If the verb to be used does not have an auxiliary, some part of the verb *do* is used as the interrogative signal.

Statement: Many people read the *New York Times*.
Question: Do many people read the *New York Times*?

In older English the verb regularly preceded the subject in the asking of a question without the aid of an auxiliary:

> Comes he often?
> Wreaks he heavy vengeance?
> Drives he a hard bargain?

This pattern, except for some uses of poetry and a rare occurrence in prose, has faded from common use. But if the verb is some part of *to be* (occasionally *to have*) the simple inversion still applies:

> Is he not skillful?
> Were they conquerors?
> Has no one a pencil? or
> Does no one have a pencil?

Inverted order is an important aspect of interrogation in English sentence patterns, but as we have seen, it is not essential to the asking of a question.

Still another inversion providing variety in running prose is accomplished by the opening of a sentence with an adverb or an adverbial phrase:

> Never can I finish this task.
> By the side of the road stood an ancient inn.
> Ever after flew the banner of freedom.

From all the preceding illustrations the fact should strike home that English communication is performed in sentences which by and large follow a regular pattern which rules the majority of statements, namely, the S-V-O pattern. But within this pattern very great variety is possible because of the types of subjects, verbs, and objects available, and because of the great variety of modifiers to be inserted where needed. Hence the fixed pattern is not a rigid mold so much as a basic skeleton to support many outward forms. Nevertheless, English idiom also permits a number of inversions of the basic pattern to signal a certain kind of communication, such as a question, or to bring about emphasis and variety. Just as in the music we most admire a certain amount of syncopation relieves the steady underlying rhythm without replacing it, so in English prose the inversions from the basic sentence pattern provide pleasing variety without destroying the strength and vigor of a regular pattern. Our next consideration is the variety and interest further created by word order within the basic pattern.

In summarizing modern English word order, Professor Curme says, "The normal word order has become the form of expression suited to the mind in its normal condition of steady activity and easy movement, from which it only departs under the stress of emotion, or for logical reasons, or in conformity to strict rules." [2]

WORD ORDER OF MODIFYING ELEMENTS

The two chief modifying elements in the English language are called *adjectives* and *adverbs*. These modifiers may be employed as single words, phrases, or clauses. Their positions in sentences vary greatly from the almost fixed pattern of the single word adjective, to the almost complete freedom of position of certain adverbs. Part of the skill in the production of effective English sentences lies in knowing how to place modifiers according to two basic requirements:

a. To place fixed modifiers where they belong.
b. To place movable modifiers where they best express the shade of meaning desired.

Adjective Modifiers

a. The single word adjective. Examples:

> *Three tall* boys put up the decorations.
> It was a *clear, breezy* day
> Bring me the *five-inch* wrench.
> Professor Jones gave a *long* but *interesting* talk.

It is obvious at once that the simple adjective stands before the noun it modifies and almost never appears anywhere else. A few

[2] George O. Curme, *Syntax* (Boston, D. C. Heath and Co., 1931), p. 351.

inversions survive as special formulas but do not set a pattern of free use. It is customary in English to say *attorney-general, castle royal, a servant true and loyal, nothing green,* and so on, but these are distinctly felt to be special cases which do not permit such parallels as *cheese Swiss, a horse black, a stroke effective.*

   b. The adjective phrase. Examples:

> Preposition: The house *by the side of the road.*
> Participle: *Having completed his task,* the boy . . .
> Infinitive: Boats *to rent* are. . . .

Note first that the prepositional phrase itself is one of the most rigid patterns in English. It almost never deviates from the formula preposition + modifier + object. Wherever it may appear in the sentence, and whether adjective or adverb, it follows the same fixed pattern.

The prepositional phrase as adjective almost invariably follows the noun that it modifies. In this it exactly reverses the pattern of the simple adjective. Hence we say *a big house, a steel bridge,* but *a house of great size, a bridge of steel.* This variation of pattern is useful in avoiding the dullness of a long string of nouns preceded by adjectives.

The participial phrase quite generally precedes the noun it modifies, but may also follow it. The speaker or writer may freely choose the position of the participial phrase. Examples:

> The boy, having finished his work, went home.
> Having finished his work, the boy went home.
> The boy went home, having finished his work.

The infinitive as adjective is not common, but when it is used it tends to follow the noun it modifies.

   c. The adjective clause. Examples:

> The girl *who sang* is my cousin.
> This decision, *which was absurd,* led to our driving many extra
>   miles without dinner.
> Tom, *whose turn it was,* took the wheel.
> This is the wheel *that needs the grease.*

As can be seen in these examples, the adjective clause generally follows the noun that it modifies. In common speech it is sometimes delayed, usually at a loss in clarity. Compare the sentence above with this variation: "This decision led to our driving many miles without dinner, *which was absurd*." Because of the feeling in English that an adjective modifies the noun that it follows, such postponement of the modifier confuses the meaning, to ultimate absurdities like "He sold the piano from the factory which had square legs." Similar difficulties occur when an adjective clause is used to modify a general idea rather than a specific noun, as in "He looked down the barrel of the gun, which was foolish." The meaning is reasonably clear, but the feeling in English that an adjective clause modifies the noun it follows gives a touch of absurdity to this sentence and others like it.

Adverb Modifiers

Unlike the adjective modifiers, which tend to have a fixed position with regard to the words they modify, the adverb modifiers are fairly movable and accomplish their task of modification when placed before or after the words they modify, and even when rather widely removed from the words to be modified. Part of the pleasing variety to be accomplished within the S-V-O pattern of the English sentence is effected by the free placement of adverbs, whether word, phrase, or clause.

   a. The single word adverb. Examples:

> Please come *soon*.
> *Quickly* the train crossed the bridge.
> The speaker had traveled *extensively*.
> *Obviously* no one was *there*.

Certain adverbs, such as *quickly, quietly, generally, possibly,* and many others, are extremely free in placement and may occur anywhere in the sentence so long as they do not break into other more fixed combinations. For example:

Quickly the train crossed the bridge.
The train *quickly* crossed the bridge.
The train crossed *quickly* the bridge. (possible but not usual)
The train crossed the bridge *quickly*.

Other adverbs, such as *only*, *truly*, *naturally*, may occur at various points in a sentence, but by position they indicate shades of meaning. Consequently their position is dictated by the shade of meaning intended. Examples:

1. *Only* he could do this task.
2. He *only* could do this task.
3. He could *only* do this task.
4. He could do *only* this task.
5. He could do this task *only*.

Example 1 emphasizes the subject and indicates that this subject alone could perform the action. Example 2 is ambiguous; it could convey the intention of Example 1 or of 3. Example 3 suggests that the subject can perform but this one action, but is still a trifle ambiguous. Examples 4 and 5 unequivocally limit the subject to the performance of a particular action. Because of the logical ambiguity that can occur by the placement of these adverbs, the older grammar books presented rules to restrict the placement of such adverbs as *only*. These rules were never strictly followed and today are generally ignored. One will hear or read, "He only had five dollars" more often than, "He had only five dollars." But when *only* precedes the subject, it usually limits the subject and not the verb, and is therefore an adjective, as in "Only he had five dollars." But note that in "*Only* he remained," *only* might be considered an adverb, despite its position.

   b. The adverbial phrase. Examples:

      Mrs. Smith came *by airplane*.
      The messenger hurried *to the bank*.
      At the side door was a potted palm.

With verbs of action the adverbial phrase usually follows the verb. When it begins the sentence it often produces an inversion, as in

"To the bank hurried the messenger," or as in the third example above. As in the single word adverb, the placement of some adverbial phrases produces shades of meaning. Note the difference of significance between "*In time* I shall finish" and "I shall finish *in time.*" The first conveys a sense of an indefinite future, while the second indicates a specific moment. The effective employment of such subtleties of meaning can be a delight to writer and reader.

What is commonly called the "indirect object" may be considered here. It may be expressed in the form of a prepositional phrase or without a preposition. When the preposition is omitted, the placement of the phrase or word is absolutely fixed; it must appear after the verb and before the direct object. Examples:

> Tom gave *Jack* a catcher's mitt.
> Some teachers give *children* homework.
> Please give *me* a second chance.

When the preposition is used, the indirect object is in the form of an adverbial phrase and usually follows the direct object, though not invariably. Examples:

> Mary, take some bread crumbs *to the birds.*
> The manager gave an extra tire *to the motorist.*
> The Chamber of Commerce gave *to the school* a handsome emblem.

(But note in modern British use the indirect object *after* the direct object, as in "Henry gave it me.")

> *c. The adverbial clause.* Examples:
>
>> *When your work is finished,* please bring it to me.
>> The child stayed home *because he was sick.*
>> The captain, *while his men slept,* examined their rifles and equipment.
>> This argumentative speaker takes, *whenever he can,* an opposite point of view.

From these examples it is clear that the adverbial clause is very free and may occur in many parts of the sentence. It may precede or follow any part of the S-V-O structure. This freedom of position is a valuable aid to the creation of variety and interest within the basic S-V-O pattern and in the common inversions. (Whitehall asserts, "The tremendous flexibility of the English sentence is largely made possible by the various positions open to the movable modifiers." [3])

THE POSITION OF CONNECTIVES

Such conjunctions as *and, but, still, yet,* and so on stand between the elements they join and cannot be moved from this position without obscuring the meaning. Despite popular ideas to the contrary, they may be used to open sentences and, indeed, frequently do so. Obviously the sentence so introduced must warrant the conjunction by a direct relationship of meaning to the previous sentence.

Examples:

> From all sides came the indignant protests of individuals and groups whose sense of justice was outraged. *And* these voices swelled to a mighty chorus.
>
> Extravagant offers were made to any person who might solve the baffling problem. *But* no solution was ever presented.

The only warning necessary with regard to the use of *and, but,* and other co-ordinating conjunctions at the opening of sentences is that they are best used sparingly, because of the heavy emphasis they create when introducing a new sentence.

Adverbial subordinating words, such as *while, where, when, as, if, because, for,* always precede the predication which they introduce. But such adverbial connectives as *however, moreover, notwithstanding, nevertheless* are placed rather freely in the predication which they modify. Examples:

> No business was completed; *nevertheless,* the meeting was considered a success.

[3] Harold Whitehall, *Structural Essentials of English* (New York, Harcourt, Brace and Co., 1956), p. 47.

His success was greeted with applause; his friends, *moreover*, felt that he richly deserved the award.

A general invitation to the lecture was issued. Not a single person outside the class came, *however*.

SUBORDINATION

A leading characteristic of modern English prose is the tendency to construct sentences in which several associated ideas are attached to or subordinated to a leading idea. It is not too great an exaggeration to say that skill in subordination is the first requisite of a successful writer of our times. In earlier English, subordination was not so fully expected. Ideas were associated by juxtaposition rather than by subordination. Note this characteristic passage from the 17th Chapter of the Gospel according to St. Matthew (English prose of approximately 1611): "And after six days Jesus taketh Peter, James, and John his brother, and bringeth them up into an high mountain apart, and was transfigured before them: and his face did shine as the sun, and his raiment was white as light. And behold, there appeared unto them Moses, and Elias talking with him."

It would not be unusual in modern English prose to find the five predications of the passage above placed into one sentence with varying degrees of subordination, as, for example: "After six days Jesus, taking Peter, James, and his brother John, brought them up into a high mountain where He was transfigured before them, His face shining as the sun, His raiment white as light, whereupon appeared Moses and Elias in conversation."

In this version only one independent predication survives, *Jesus ... brought them*, modified by the subordinate predications *whereupon appeared ... in conversation*, and *where he was transfigured*. The remaining ideas are expressed in participial phrases and one elliptical clause, *his raiment white as light*.

The point of this illustration is to indicate a change of style in English sentence structure. The student who writes "We took a trip Sunday and we went to the beach, we sure had a good time the water was just right everybody went swimming" is unconsciously employing an older style in English in which ideas were related to each other largely by being placed side by side. Modern English prose, perhaps as a reflection of its greater artistic maturity, expects ideas to be related to each other within the sentence structure by subordination to dependent clauses, participial phrases, and phrasal or single word modifiers. Developing writers can profit from a frequent review of the table of subordination, which might be presented with these illustrations:

TABLE OF SUBORDINATION

1. No subordination: The treasurer's report was carefully drawn up. It covered five pages of typed paper.
2. Subordination by clause: The treasurer's report, *which covered five pages of typed paper*, was carefully drawn up.
3. Subordination by participial phrase: The treasurer's report, *covering five pages of typed paper*, was carefully drawn up.
4. Subordination by modifying phrase: *The carefully drawn up* report of the treasurer covered five pages of typed paper.
5. Subordination by single word modifier: The *five-page* report of treasurer was carefully drawn up; or The treasurer's *meticulous* report covered five pages of typed paper.
6. Subordination by apposition: The treasurer's report, *five typed pages*, was carefully drawn up.

PARALLEL STRUCTURE

Consistent with the reduction of predications in the condensed style of modern English prose is the extensive use of parallel structure. The virtue of parallelism is its function of permitting a number of related materials to be incorporated into the frame of a single sentence pattern. Any part of a sentence can be split up or built up into parallel parts: subject, verb, complements, and modifiers, from single word to extended clauses, may be divided into parallel segments. The effect is to accomplish an economy of structure which clarifies meaning and is pleasing to reader or listener. Of prime importance in the teaching of such structures as the participial phrase, the gerund phrase, the infinitive phrase, the absolute phrase, and others is to show the ability of these structures to create interesting and economical sentences by arranging parallel sequences of a given structure. Some examples of parallel structure follow:

> *The prepositional phrase:* I am convinced of your improvement by your good conduct, by your attention to your studies, and by your evident desire to please your mother.
>
> *The participial phrase:* Having checked every part of the engine, having tested the spark plugs and coils, and having assured myself of the supply of oil and water, I gave the word to load the truck and start it on its journey.
>
> *The infinitive phrase:* From an early age the naturalist had made it his habit to observe closely what happened in his garden, to collect copious notes from his observations, and to draw conclusions which might direct his further work.
>
> *The modifying clause:* I urged him to donate his time to the Red Cross while he was still free, while his interest in the work was high, and while he could profit most from the experience it would provide.

Students may be helped at first to see the parallel nature of these structures by simple diagrammatic representation. The sentence above, for example, could be set out thus:

I urged him to donate his time to the Red Cross—

when?	while he was still free
	while his interest in the work was high
	while he could profit most, etc.

After the analysis of a number of structures employing parallelism in various parts of the sentence, students can develop skill in this structure from exercises requiring the completion of parallel parts:

A swimmer	who has practiced faithfully who _____ and who _____	may fully expect to win his race.

Harriet was puzzled about	what to wear to the junior prom _____ _____

An alert teacher will watch for the use of parallel structures in students' writing, will read aloud good examples from composition papers, and will encourage further use by judicious praise and commendation. (Note parallel structure!)

Because subordination and parallel structure play such an important part in the syntax of modern English, the teaching of writing must lay stress upon the means by which each is accomplished. It is to these ends that the teaching of grammar should be directed. To use subordination and parallel syntax the student will need to know the names of the kinds of structures available to him and how they are formed. This kind of instruction is truly grammar; these outcomes are the reasons for teaching grammar; and the success of students in creating condensed, interesting sentences is the measure of success in such instruction.

REFERENCES

BRYANT, Margaret M., *Modern English and Its Heritage* (New York, The Macmillan Co., 1948).

BRYANT, Margaret M., and AIKEN, Janet Rankin, *Psychology of English* (New York, Columbia University Press, 1940).

CURME, George Oliver, *Syntax* (Boston, D. C. Heath and Co., 1931).

FRIES, Charles C., *The Structure of English* (New York, Harcourt, Brace and Co., 1952).

LLOYD, Donald J., and WARFEL, Harry R., *American English in Its Cultural Setting* (New York, Alfred A. Knopf, 1956).

ROBERTS, Paul, *Patterns of English* (New York, Harcourt, Brace and Co., 1956).

WHITEHALL, Harold, *Structural Essentials of English* (New York, Harcourt, Brace and Co., 1956).

IX

Observations on the Teaching of English Grammar

FROM THE HISTORICAL OUTLINE of the development of grammar in Western civilization in earlier chapters of this book, it is clear that the term *grammar* has meant various things at various times, and sometimes several things at one time. This plurality of meaning is characteristic of the present time and is the source of confusions in the discussion of grammar as part of the education of children and youth. If one teacher should say, "I do not favor teaching any grammar before the seventh grade, and not much then," another is likely to reply, "But if you do not, how will your students learn to capitalize correctly, to punctuate sentences, or to spell accurately?" A third is almost sure to remark, "If you teach no grammar, how can you expect to have correct usage in speech and writing?"

The confusions as to what grammar is and what it may be expected to do have much to do with the current dissatisfactions with the teaching of grammar. If a general agreement could be reached as to what grammar is, and what it can be properly expected to do in the education of youth, a long step forward in the problem of teaching grammar will be taken.

Because the remainder of this book deals with the applications of grammar to the instruction of young people in the use of their language, it is important to make clear exactly how such terms as grammar and usage are to be used in the following chapters, and to explain the reasons for the specific definitions adopted for this treatment.

BASIC DEFINITIONS

Let us define grammar as *the study of the way a language is used; English grammar is the study of how English is used*. In other words, grammar is the observation of the forms and arrangements of English words as they are employed singly and in combination to convey meaning in discourse. In this definition of grammar the expressions "I ain't got no books," and "We seen him when he done it," are as grammatical as "I have no books," and "We saw him when he did it." Both kinds of expressions are examples of how English is used to convey meaning. The fact that we may prefer one kind of expression over another has nothing to do with grammar as it is here defined. Consequently we shall rule out such terms as "good grammar" or "bad grammar" and speak only of a grammar which describes what happens when English is used.

When we look more closely, we shall find this term *grammar* covers two main types of language phenomena: changes which occur in the structure of words themselves, and changes which occur in the placing of words into meaningful groups. The first type we see in the examples *rose, roses*, in *I, me, we, us*, and so on, and in *sink, sank, sunk*. This kind of grammar deals with the shapes of words, and is appropriately named *morphology*, from a Greek word which means shape. It is the function of morphology to study the changes which occur in the form of English words, and to explain the relationship between these changes and meaning. A brief history of English forms is presented in Chapter VII.

The second type of phenomena, the changes which occur in the order in which words are placed to convey meaning, is called syntax. It is the function of syntax to study the order of words in meaningful discourse and to attempt to explain the relationship between word order and meaning. The fact that this is not always easy to do only adds to the significance of the endeavor. What is commonly called sentence structure is the observation of how words go together to form conventional patterns: the subject-verb-object pattern of the common English statement is one example; the fact that the English adjective almost invariably precedes the noun it modifies is another. Patterns of word order are analyzed in Chapter VIII.

One of the interesting developments in the English language is the gradual shift from reliance upon morphology to express grammatical relationships which in turn determine meanings, to reliance upon word order or syntax. Thus the meanings of a noun in a sentence, which once were expressed by changes in the form of the word, usually by endings, are now expressed in English generally by the use of such prepositions as *of, to, from, by,* and others. The expression of time relationships in English verbs other than simple past time is accomplished by the addition of auxiliaries, which form verb phrases. Even the simple present tense of most verbs is now a phrase, as in "I am speaking," rather than "I speak." Future time is indicated by a wide variety of word patterns. Because of this growth of importance of the groupings and arrangements of words, it is well to speak of grammar today as concerned with what remains of the morphological changes in English words, and with the very great current significance of the order of words.

Grammar, then, is structure; the observation of what people do when they use English words in discourse. Grammar, as here defined, makes no choices, expresses no preferences, takes no sides, creates no standards. It endeavors to see English as it is in an objective, scientific manner. The fact that the scheme of grammar we now use is poorly fitted for such an endeavor is one of the problems in the teaching of grammar. Some of the efforts to devise a more scientific scheme of English grammar are described in Chapter VI. The traditional terminology has been used in this book, with some modifications to avoid the most glaring faults of conventional English grammar.

Usage, on the other hand, is the term employed to cover the full range of choice and discrimination in the use of language. Usage makes choices, expresses preferences, takes sides, creates standards. The bases upon which choices are made, preferences are expressed, sides are taken, and standards are set up is the concern of usage. Usage is to grammar as etiquette is to behavior. Behavior simply notes what people do; etiquette sets a stamp of approval or disapproval upon actions, or sets up standards to guide actions. The specific business of usage, therefore, is to determine what choices and discriminations are made in the use of English, and then to analyze the forces, social and psychological, which determine the choices. In practical terms, usage is the study which notes the variety of choices made in the use of English, observes the standards set up by such choices or created to influence such choices, and attempts to evaluate the validity of such standards.

GRAMMAR AND USAGE

The distinction between grammar and usage as defined above is not generally recognized in theory or observed in practice in current education. On the contrary, a very real confusion concerning these two elements of language teaching results in obscurity of aim and lack of success in the language teaching activities of the classroom. There is, of course, a close relationship between grammar and usage in those cases where the propriety of use of a certain word form is governed by the history of its grammatical forms. For example, the past tense form of the verb *stick* is *stuck* because of the history of the development of this verb. The irregular form *stuck* can be explained by reference to historical grammar. But when a fifth-grade child says or writes *sticked* as the past tense of *stick*, he is following the same process which produced such current past tense forms as *helped* or *wept* from verbs which once had a change of vowel in the past tense. To correct the child at the moment of his use of *sticked* calls for a consideration of propriety —that is, usage—rather than of grammatical history. The grammatical explanation may interest him but it is not likely to influence his speech habits. What he needs to know at the moment is that *sticked* is used only by children or very uneducated adults, and that he will be expected to say and write the form *stuck*. This form of instruction should be called usage rather than grammar.

There is a popular and apparently almost indestructible idea that the study of grammar is essential to the development of good usage in children and youth. Specifically, teachers believe that the child who says or writes "We done it" will be corrected to say and write thereafter "We did it" by learning the principal parts of the verb *to do*. There is no convincing evidence that such learning takes place. On the contrary, there is overwhelming evidence that pupils who are carefully coached on the principal parts of irregular verbs in English classrooms cheerfully continue to maltreat these verbs in speech and writing.

The point that is not clear, but that this book would like to emphasize, is that usage instruction is chiefly habit breaking and habit forming, and derives its instructional methods from the science of human behavior. In simple terms, correction and practice in corrected responses is the proper technique. Knowledge of forms and grammatical history plays a negligible part in this process. On the other hand, the building of sentences and the manipulation of sentence materials for improved style are at the very center of grammar instruction and are the chief reason for the teaching of grammar. In the subsequent discussion of the teaching of grammar the term will mean the structure of English expression. All matters concerned with propriety, word choice, idiom, and the like will be called usage. The fundamental assumption is that grammar teaches the form and structure of English sentences; usage teaches correctness and propriety in word and phrase. These two phases of language, while related, are not the same, and are taught by differing approaches and methods.

CLASSIFICATION BY FUNCTION

It was characteristic of nineteenth-century grammar to lay great stress on the classification of the words which are used to form sentences, and to require not only the memorization of definitions of the parts of speech but also the recognition of many subcategories. Nouns, for example, were classified as common and proper, concrete and abstract, collective, and so on; adverbs were classified in terms of time, place, manner, quantity, quality; verbs had to be identified as copulative, transitive, intransitive, and so forth; indeed, all parts of speech were not only specifically defined but were divided into a number of categories which the student was expected to learn and apply to the analysis of words in sentences.

In recent decades the emphasis on the subcategories has faded to a considerable extent, though some vestiges of it remain in current grammar books. But the grammars of today still define parts of speech a priori; that is, they assume that words belong to parts of speech by natural classification and are to be identified as so belonging. Thus the word *home* is to be classified as a noun, as it is in the sentence "You have a beautiful *home*." But what is it in these sentences: "I went *home* early," "*Home* handicrafts declined in the eighteenth century," "The bird has a *homing* instinct"? Obviously the category of noun will not serve for these, and to call the word by the name of any other part of speech would do violence to the system of classification. Because of the flexibility of English words, moving easily from one part of speech to another, the arbitrary classification of parts of speech has long been recognized as unsatisfactory. Nevertheless, up to the present, so far as the standard textbooks are concerned it prevails, but with a kind of tacit understanding that it is partly fiction.

Modern linguistic scholars are agreed that parts of speech cannot be used to classify words prior to the appearance of the words in sentences. Words are to be classified only as they are used in the particular situation under observation. From this point on the experts differ widely as to the terms to use for classification, but they are agreed on the approach. Some use the traditional names of the parts of speech with fresh applications, as in the following illustration:

Mode of definition: All the following are morphological plus syntactic definitions. By this I mean that in every case "when used in a sentence" is a part of the definition and words to be tested are to be substituted in the places where the model words regularly appear. The apparently childish repetition of an admonition is very necessary. It should be memorized as a part of each definition and never omitted.

1. *Noun.* A noun is a word that behaves in a sentence like the word *blackness.* No word is a noun outside of a sentence and in and of itself.

2. *Verb.* A verb is a word that behaves in a sentence like the word *blacken.* No word is a verb outside of a sentence and in and of itself.

3. *Pronoun.* A pronoun is one of the following words (I/me, you, he/she/it/him/her, we/us, they/them, who/whom) when used in a sentence in its normal way. No word is a pronoun outside of a sentence and in and of itself.

4. *Adjective.* An adjective is a word that behaves in a sentence like the word *blackish.* No word is an adjective outside of a sentence and in and of itself.

5. *Adverb.* An adverb is a word that behaves in a sentence like the word *blackishly.* No word is an adverb outside a sentence and in and of itself.

6. *Preposition.* The following words are prepositions when used in a sentence without extra emphasis. When they bear emphasis they are probably adverbs. (Give list to be memorized.) No word is a preposition outside a sentence and in and of itself.

7. *Interjection.* An interjection is a single word followed by a double barred juncture where a continuation signal is normal. No word is an interjection outside the stream of speech, a person talking, and it is an interjection when used as described above and only then. [1]

In an earlier chapter the scheme of Fries has been analyzed

[1] James A. Walker, unpublished report prepared for the meeting of the CCCC, March, 1956. Used by permission of the author.

(Chapter VI, p. 63) to show his method of identifying the four formal speech elements which he refers to as classes 1, 2, 3, and 4. Class 1 words, for example, are those which will fit into such frames as (The) _____ was good; (the) _____s were good; (the) _____ remembered (the) _____; (the) _____ went there. Whitehall (Chapter VI, p. 69) uses the traditional names for the parts of speech, does not define them, but shows through their position and use in sentences what they are. Roberts (Chapter VI, p. 70) uses the four form classes of Fries, but calls them nouns, verbs, adjectives, and adverbs. His definition of a noun is: "A *noun* is a word like *apple, beauty,* or *desk.* That is, it is a word that patterns as *apple, beauty,* or *desk* do. It is a word that occurs in positions like those in which *apple, beauty,* and *desk* occur." [2]

These illustrations serve to show the trend toward avoiding definitions of parts of speech other than upon terms of pattern or function in sentences. In the teaching of English grammar in junior and senior high school, the difficulties of classification can be avoided by permitting the concept of noun, verb, adjective, adverb, and so on to develop by observation of these forms in their functional positions in sentences rather than by any a priori definitions.

CORRECTIVE VS. CONSTRUCTIVE GRAMMAR

The story of the development of English grammar and its use as a school subject in the United States makes evident the transmission of an attitude toward grammar derived from the eighteenth century, expanded in the nineteenth century, and continuing on in the twentieth, despite the opposition of linguists on the one hand, and practical classroom educators on the other hand. This attitude may be put in these general terms: "English, as it is currently used, is full of errors. The grammarians know these errors and are determined to correct them. The purpose of the teaching of grammar is to eliminate errors." This attitude, though unsound

[2] Paul Roberts, *Patterns of English* (New York, Harcourt, Brace and Co., 1956), p. 13.

from many points of view, persists despite the efforts of scholars and leading teachers of English to abolish it, and to substitute a recognition of grammar as a tool to the effective expression of English in sentences. As a result the teacher of English, through misguided zeal, spends the major part of his time and energy on the correction of error at the expense of the real purpose of language instruction, which is communication.

The "errors" of eighteenth-century grammarians were drawn largely from the writings of previous and contemporary authors and included a few variations which neither usage nor the history of the language could very strongly support; but on the whole the "errors" were (1) variations fully justified by normal changes in the language as it was used; (2) variants derived from the simplification of the morphology of English, such as is represented by the alternate past tense forms of the verb *to sink:* either *sank* or *sunk;* (3) pairs of words whose usage was by no means so specialized as the reformers would have it, such as: *farther, further;* or (4) just plain ordinary prejudice on the part of the reformer, as in the condemnation of the participle *proven*. From such petty tampering with English grew the conviction that the main purpose of English teaching is to discover how many variants from a fixed and arbitrary standard of correctness a student may employ, and to attack these variations as morally sinful deviations whose correction is the main business of the teacher of English. This attitude, reaching its peak in mid-nineteenth century, persists into our own times. It is evidenced by two features of current materials used by English teachers: the heavy dosage of formal grammar in the textbooks for the upper elementary grades and the junior high school, and the distressing proliferation of so-called workbooks whose emphasis is upon the mass correction of errors which occur more in the unhappy minds of the workbook authors than they do in the normal communication of students. Thus the reformers' hands still lie heavy upon us in making rules and corrections the center of English language instruction in the place of creative, meaningful exchange of ideas in a language pattern tolerant of variations inherent in the natural use of English.

But in the nineteenth century the corrective attitude did not go unchallenged. The attack came on one side from practical educators, who could not fail to note the sterile futility of attempting to teach the functional use of a living language through the memorization of rules whose comprehension was often beyond the powers of the students who were supposed to learn them. Nor could such practical teachers ignore the fact that many of the corrections of English offered in the textbooks were contrary to their own speech habits and those of their educated friends. From these educators, then, came the impetus toward the reduction of grammatical instruction to that which was functional in the daily needs of language, and the beginnings of a doubt as to whether all the so-called errors were actually errors after all.

The attack on prescriptive grammar came even more strongly from the scholars who were engaged in the new and exciting study of general linguistics. From scattered beginnings in the early nineteenth century, a slow but steady body of knowledge concerning the nature of language and the history of languages was accumulating. From the patient work of many investigators the story of the origins, growth, changes, and development of the western European languages unfolded and led to generalizations about language, grammar, and usage widely different from those previously held. The application of such work, as it has influenced the teaching of the English language in schools, is to be found in Chapter 12 of *The English Language Arts*, the report of the Curriculum Commission of the National Council of Teachers of English, designed to provide the background of beliefs and practices to guide the teachers of the United States in the making of English curriculums.

From this report, note the following quotation:

In the last half century linguists who have devoted themselves to the study of the English language have evolved five basic concepts which are, or should be, the foundation of the current attitude toward any teaching of the English language today:

1. Language changes constantly.
2. Change in language is normal.
3. The spoken language is *the* language.
4. Correctness rests upon usage.
5. All usage is relative. [3]

These principles of language study create a set of attitudes toward language and usage entirely different from the point of view which was developed in the eighteenth century and carried forward through the nineteenth. In the historical portion of this book we have seen how the popular conception of grammar confused the issues of recording and analyzing the behavior of a language with the function of setting standards and determining usage in the language. In the popular mind today this confusion still persists, but among teachers of English at least it is giving way to a clearer recognition of the separate functions of grammar and usage. Increasingly, as this distinction becomes accepted, instruction in grammar will emphasize the patterns of English construction which serve to bring about effective communication. Usage will be concerned with the bases by which discrimination among uses of language may be made and will attempt to indicate what variations of expression are acceptable for various kinds of communication. Such a distinction should make much easier the creation of curriculums in grammar for the specific purpose of improving sentence structure and programs of usage analysis which assist the student to develop discrimination in the use of English so that he may express himself effectively in all the common affairs of life.

The foregoing discussion should make clear that what is most needed in the teaching of English grammar and usage is a new point of view or a change of attitude. In simple terms, it should be our goal to escape as much as possible from the long-established

[3] *The English Language Arts,* The Commission on the English Curriculum of the National Council of the Teachers of English (New York, Appleton-Century-Crofts, Inc., 1952).

tradition that the English teacher's primary task is to preserve some mythical purity of the English language by teaching "correctness," and to adopt as a working principle the view that English is of chief value not for what it was or is, but for what it can do in the communication of ideas.

REFERENCES

Curriculum Commission, National Council of Teachers of English, *The English Language Arts* (New York, Appleton-Century-Crofts, Inc., 1952).

FRIES, Charles C., *The Structure of English* (New York, Harcourt, Brace and Co., 1952).

ROBERTS, Paul, *Patterns of English* (New York, Harcourt, Brace and Co., 1956).

WHITEHALL, Harold, *Structural Essentials of English* (New York, Harcourt, Brace and Co., 1956).

X

Teaching Language in the Elementary School

THROUGHOUT THE PRESENT CHAPTER the term *the elementary school* will be taken to mean the kindergarten plus grades one through six, inclusive. While it is true that a very large number of elementary schools include also grades seven and eight, from the point of view of curriculum it is desirable to deal with the first six grades as a unit, and to associate grades seven and eight with the junior high school curriculum, regardless of the physical location of the classes. This separation is particularly significant in the discussion of grammar, inasmuch as current practice tends to regard the seventh grade as the point at which a serious consideration of structural grammar should begin.

The teaching of the language arts in the elementary grades is the task of picking up the child's language skills which he brings from his home environment, adapting them to the wider demands of enlarging social contacts, and improving them in quantity and quality to develop adequately the child's performance in speaking and writing, listening and reading, required of him for continued success in school and in his social and personal life outside of school. The processes for such a task must of necessity be creative and functional rather than analytical and normative. In other words, in the elementary grades the major emphasis will be upon the actual use of language and the improvement of skills through use, rather than upon knowledge about the language itself and attention to restrictive rules. In curriculum terms the foregoing generalization would indicate that grammar of the analytical and structural sort will have little or no place in the elementary grades, but that the oral and written conventions of English, those which function in actual speaking and writing, will be of chief concern. Associated with the learning and practicing of these conventions will be a developmental program of word usage instruction to replace childish or substandard usages with those appropriate to the expanding social responsibilities of the child. In the simplest way to state the point of view, "language" in the elementary grades means a growing command of the patterns and manners of speech, an introduction to and development of the patterns and forms of writing, and increasing maturity and discrimination in word usage. The kind of instruction needed to bring about these skills must take into account how English is commonly spoken and written.

PATTERNS IN ORAL ENGLISH

Of first importance in the description of how English is used is the recognition of those patterns or formulas which by custom and habit characterize the process of communication. Taken by themselves such words and phrases as *Hello, How do you do? How are you? Good-bye, See you soon,* and so forth may seem empty of meaning, but they are really the small change of social contacts, opening the way to more meaningful exchanges of ideas among the speakers. The adult or child who lacks ease in these convenient oral formulas is embarrassed, tongue-tied, and awkward where he could otherwise be at ease. Consequently, it is part of the training in speaking to teach these social phrases in connection with the social situations in which they occur, with enough practice to insure their automatic appearance where needed.

These patterns extend to the activities of greeting and parting from friends and acquaintances, answering the door bell, using the telephone, taking messages for a member of the family, excusing oneself from the table, the room, or from a group, interrupting someone who is speaking, getting attention where necessary, and making introductions. The latter are particularly important in the creation of ease for further speech. Children need to learn and practice patterns like "John, this is my sister Sue," "Bill, meet my friend Henry," "Mother, this is Betsy from my class at school," "Miss Anderson, may I introduce my mother?" [1]

These social patterns are truly basic in teaching how English is used, and should be practiced frequently until each child is reasonably adept at using the correct pattern for various social occasions. These opening conventions lead naturally to the skills of discussion, which include waiting one's turn to speak, gaining the attention of the leader or of the group, speaking briefly and to the point, correcting the error or misstatement of another with courtesy, quoting or citing an authority correctly, and learning to summarize what has been discussed. For the upper elementary grades these patterns of speech behavior lead to the conventions of a formal meeting, such as addressing the chair, waiting to be recognized, making or seconding a motion, making statements clearly and briefly, and bringing business to a conclusion. These matters not only develop language readiness in the individual but they promote the exchange of ideas in society.

THE PROBLEM OF GOOD USAGE

From their homes, children bring to school a wide assortment of speech habits from various levels of usage. Children from homes where cultivated speech prevails, where usage errors have been corrected since infancy, need no school attention except to protect them from the unconscious adoption of less desirable forms from their associates. Others, less fortunate in background, bring to school speech patterns and habits which do not measure up to the expectations of school and society beyond the home. A very large

[1] Delia E. Kibbe, Lou LaBrant, and Robert C. Pooley, *Handbook of English for Boys and Girls* (Chicago, Scott, Foresman and Co., 1939), pp. 9–20.

number of children fall into this latter group, necessitating specific attention to the breaking of less desirable speech habits and the substitution of those more acceptable. The goal is easy, informal, acceptable English. No one questions this goal, but opinions differ as to the way to accomplish it.

Many teachers feel that correction is best accomplished by teaching grammatical terminology and structure. The child who says "I seen you" must be taught the principal parts of the verb *to see*. He will thus discover that *seen* is a past participle, not a past tense, and the form that he wants is *saw*. Having learned these facts he will thereafter (his teacher hopes) always avoid *seen* except as a past participle, and will say "I saw you." There is little evidence to support the transfer of factual knowledge of grammatical forms to the speech habits of children. This fact leads other teachers to place greater reliance upon repetition and practice with desirable forms, especially ear practice, leaving grammatical explanations to a later day. This contention seems to be reinforced by generally accepted principles in the psychology of learning in children, and leads to two generalizations of importance in the approach to usage in the elementary grades. These are:

1. To break bad habits and to substitute more desirable habits necessitates a very strict limitation on the number of specific items of usage to be attacked in the elementary grades.
2. The items selected for mastery must be taught soundly and thoroughly in accordance with what is known of the psychology of habit breaking and formation.

From all the evidence now available, the most effective type of usage instruction in the elementary grades lays stress upon the removal of less desirable habits by direct correction, and much oral and written practice to substitute more desirable forms. These principles underlie such instruction:

1. The number of items for specific attack will be kept as small as possible. [2]

[2] See Robert C. Pooley, *Teaching English Usage* (New York, Appleton-Century-Crofts, Inc., 1946), p. 180, for a list prepared by teachers.

2. Only speech forms which are frequent in occurrence, and which are unquestionably outside the limits of informal standard speech, will be attacked.

3. Once an item has been selected for correction, no exceptions will be tolerated. This means that both teacher and pupil must be alert to catch and correct any lapses from the desired form. For example: *He give it to me* for *He gave it to me.* This use of *give*, once made the subject of attack, must not be allowed to pass in *any* situation from idle chatter to formal report.

4. Specific oral drill upon desired expressions will attempt to anticipate errors. Practice upon such expressions as *I have done my work, I have seen my friend, he ran to the store, they have gone* will establish familiarity with desired patterns and will provide a positive approach to corrections. [3]

In the earlier grades particularly, great importance rests upon the teacher's skill in securing the willing response of pupils. Corrections that are made quietly, politely, and with a due regard for the feelings of the child will secure responses and results far in advance of corrections that create irritation. Certainly embarrassment and resentment should be avoided in every way. In the formation of desirable language habits the good teacher will gently lead rather than drive his pupils.

PATTERNS OF WRITTEN ENGLISH

Certain conventions of written English become familiar to the child when he first learns to write his name. He is taught and early accepts as habit that the first letter of his name is written with a capital letter, that his last name also begins with a capital letter, and if he uses an initial, that too is written as a capital letter with a period after it. (The word *written* here of course includes the block type letters used by children in the early grades.) From this

[3] See Marjorie Westcott Barrows, *Good English Through Practice* (New York, Henry Holt and Co., 1956).

start he learns to use capital letters also for the first letter of the names of his friends and for the personal pronoun *I*.

As the child undertakes to combine two or three words to write a "story," he finds that the first word of each of these groups is also a capital letter. Now a new concept appears which should soon become habit—a mark to show the end of a "story." From these foundations he acquires gradually the conventions which govern the writing of statements, questions, and exclamations. Needless to say, the development of these habits in writing should be closely linked with observation of the same conventions in his printed reading books and in blackboard exercises.

All these experiences are united in developing the first great concept of English grammar; namely, that English is written as groups of words, each group beginning with a capital letter and ending with a terminal punctuation mark: the period, the question mark, or the exclamation point. The same experiences should arouse a second observation that the other most frequently used mark of punctuation, the comma, divides or separates elements within a word group (or sentence) but never ends anything. The comma is not terminal. Although very few formal terms need to be used in establishing these customs as habits, they are, nevertheless, the very foundation of the grammar of written English. And as the sequence of these chapters will attempt to demonstrate, the chief use of grammar is to advance skills in written English.

In the elementary grades all efforts should go to the development of these habits. As the student matures and advances he will begin to see that there is a recognizable relationship between a group of words which he begins with a capital letter and ends with a terminal mark, and a unit of meaning which he intends to convey. This sense of unity of meaning will help him, without formal analysis, to become dissatisfied with a group of words whose meaning is incomplete. As he reads he will feel that "All the children" is not a complete unit of meaning whereas "All the children ran to the playground" satisfies his sense of completeness.

Similarly "Ran away" is incomplete, but "The big dog ran away" is complete. It must be clearly recognized, however, that this sense of completeness rests upon context. Thus "All the children" as a word group in isolation is not satisfying, but in response to the question, "Who ran to the playground?" the natural response, in context, is "All the children." Hence it is important in the early treatment of sentence units to distinguish between statements made in isolation of context, which must be complete, and statements, or partial word groups, in response to context, which are frequently incomplete. To insist upon full grammatical completeness for all replies to context is to create an artificiality not consistent with normal English expression. Children should certainly not be expected to acquire as habits forms of English expression which adults do not use. What the elementary grades should expect is that all complete statements, when written, shall begin with a capital letter and end with a terminal mark, and that all word groups written with a capital letter and ending with a terminal mark be complete unless clearly responding to previous context. Thus we would expect a fourth-grade child to write, "Not one of the children came to the party," when written as a statement. But in such a series as "How many children do you think came to the party? Not one!" we would accept "Not one!" as a satisfactory written unit because of its relationship to the previous context. Such tolerance is more true to English as it is customarily spoken and written than the insistence upon complete sentences in the spoken and written expression of children.

Much more difficult to overcome, and presenting a real dilemma to the teacher, is the tendency of children to group together several meaning units without terminal signs or conventional linkage. The spoken account of an experience, delivered with enthusiasm and the natural rhythms of speech, is at least tolerable. The same account when written offends the conventions. For example, a third-grade child reports with excitement and the obvious pleasure of communication, "The Smiths have a new baby he is awfully cute she let me hold him a few minutes and he began to cry so I gave him back to Mrs. Smith and he yawned." When asked to write a "story," the little girl with so interesting a piece of news is very likely to write exactly what she said. The more fluent in communication she is, the more likely she is to dash on without attention to terminal marks.

The dilemma the teacher faces is this: Is it better at this point to insist upon the formal termination of statements, in other words sentence punctuation, with the danger of cutting off the enthusiasm of real communication of ideas, or is it preferable at this stage of development to permit the child considerable latitude in the writing of statements in groups, with the danger of fixing faulty habits which may persist into high school? To this question there is no easy answer. Fluency, enthusiasm, and freedom in communication are the goals we are striving for. We want children to enjoy communicating ideas and to do so freely and easily. Since children tend to do pleasurably that in which they succeed, we want them to have pleasure and satisfaction in their written communication. There are many good arguments in favor of some freedom from formalized rules.

On the other side are equally cogent arguments. Children allowed to write extended series of statements without sentence punctuation will tend to grow increasingly indifferent to the basic character of the English written sentence. They will lose their sense of units of meaning by failing to recognize them as they write. They will be developing bad habits of unpunctuated writing which will carry over into more advanced years. Consequently they should be held responsible for formal sentence punctuation.

The dilemma can be resolved in a practical way by paying some attention to the claims of both sides. In the first three grades, while the basic conventions of written expression will be taught and practiced, children will also be encouraged to write freely and at length without excessive attention to form, other than that each written unit begin with a capital letter and end with a terminal mark. In the intermediate grades a growing attention can be directed to the sense of completeness within word groups, beginning with the incomplete, rather than the overcomplete statement. Young writers can be led to view with dissatisfaction such word groups as:

> By the end of the day.
> All the teachers and the children.
> While the rain was falling.
> Since I was unable to go.

The sense of lack of completeness in the communication of ideas which these expressions arouse, particularly when presented orally with a lack of voice drop at the end, will induce children to want to add the element which completes the statement. Frequent oral practice in finding satisfactory conclusions to incomplete ideas will result in dissatisfaction with such fragments when written. Without the use of formal grammatical terms, such practice will teach the principle that sentences beginning with a subordinate clause require an independent clause for the communication to satisfy the listener or reader.

Another difficulty of form at this period in language growth is the use of excessive co-ordination (and . . . and . . . and). In oral practice the pupil can be guided to stop and take a breath where the co-ordinating conjunction would come. Some co-ordination is naturally permissible, but its excesses should be checked. With the memory of such corrections in oral language the pupil is prepared to look upon the period as the "breath" in writing, and to break co-ordinated strings of expression by the insertion of a period and capitalization of the next word. The development of a *feeling* for such terminations is far more effective than the memorization of rules about periods and capital letters.

Somewhat more difficult to correct is the perfectly natural chain of statements known to teachers as the run-on construction: example, "We went to the County Fair it was wonderful I like the horse races best the baby pigs and lambs were cute." Since the conversation of many adults is built upon such parataxis (to use its technical name), it is not surprising that children run on in a similar manner. The conventions of acceptable English, however, require the recognition of a better handling of such groups, either by attention to formal break (periods and new sentences) or by the subordination of parts to other parts ("At the County Fair I liked the horse races best"). The suggestion of such patterns by the teacher will help the developing young writer to avoid the excessive use of run-on sentences. Some tolerance for the joining of statements can be permitted, for at the intermediate elementary stage we can scarcely expect or require absolute precision in the separation of statement units. The teacher's goal is to arouse in each student a feeling for the individual status of each statement or question. Practice in separating some groups of statements, and effectively joining others, as the children create their own little paragraphs, will furnish the most interesting and effective teaching method.

USAGE IN WRITTEN ENGLISH

When children are set the task of translating their speech into written form, they are really beginning an extremely difficult art. They will have a great deal of trouble in merely forming the letters and joining them into words which they want to state. Frequently they find it difficult even to remember the closing part of the sentence with which they start. Their attention is directed largely to mechanical matters. It is likely that whatever speech is in their minds, that speech which they have derived from their customary speech habits will be transmitted immediately into writing. The processes of writing slow down the child's expression, but at the early state, at least, they do not change it. The writing is, therefore, slower but similar to the child's speech habits. For these reasons it is clear that speech faults will carry over into writing faults. The labor of writing makes it easy for the errors which are habitual with the child to carry over into his written work. For example, if he hears at home and is accustomed to say "We was there," when he comes to write a composition in which he speaks of himself and the members of his family being at some point, he will almost surely write "We was there." On the other hand, if he has been trained by oral practice to think and to say "We were there," and has practiced this phrase in a number of classroom exercises, it will come to his mind when he is laboring with the problems of penmanship and will enable him to write "We were there." In the development of good written usage, the workbooks and practice sheets which are so customarily a part of the elementary school grammar program are of little value.

Some usage problems in written work are created by the act of writing and, therefore, have to be dealt with in connection with writing. These are generally the results of the confusing of sounds and forms in words and from the use of dialectal expressions which are perhaps habitually used by the child but are not generally approved in writing. Here are certain examples of these:

I would of come.	Who's book is this?
There (they're) too early.	I am kind a hungry.
This kind a cake.	

Fortunately there are not many specific usage problems arising from writing, so that with a little attention at the time that such errors occur in the children's early writing these can be eliminated.

STRUCTURAL KNOWLEDGE OF ENGLISH

Up to this point in our chapter the reader may wonder at the avoidance of such terms as a sentence, subject, verb, object, adjective, adverb, and the other terms that are used in organized grammar. Such avoidance has been deliberate. It is the point of view of this chapter that the foundations of spoken and written English are best laid up to and including the sixth grade without formal instruction in the terminology of grammar—that means learning the parts of speech—or in the practice of identifying and naming the various parts and functions of the sentence. This statement is based upon considerable research and background which will be summarized under the following divisions:

1. The first consideration is the question of time. Time that is used in teaching children the names of parts of speech and the identification and classification of parts of the sentence is time taken away from the practice of the skills of writing and speaking English. The modern curriculum of the elementary school is full and rich. It takes every minute of time available for the completion of the work assigned. If there were any demonstrable evidence that the teaching of grammar in the grades up to and including six resulted in superior writing and speaking on the part of the children, such instruction might be justified. However, all the evidence seems to point to the fact that skills in the use of English and practice in speaking, writing, and employing English for all the ordinary affairs of life lay a much better foundation for the child. Concentration upon the actual use of English, therefore, is much more significant and is the point of view from which this chapter is written.

2. All the evidence of research studies shows that formal grammar has very slight influence on the usage habits of children. Children learn their language by listening to their parents and by the conversation they have with other children in the home and on the playground. By the time a kindergartner reaches school, his patterns of speech are pretty well set up by his experience and have become very largely unconscious. If he has heard excellent English in his home, he speaks excellent English. If he has heard pretty good English with some minor defects, these minor defects will show up in his speech. If he has been unfortunate enough to hear regularly, "I done it," "I seen him," "Where was you," "Him and me went," and so on, he will repeat these expressions in his speech in the kindergarten. These are habits. The child is not responsible in the sense that he is doing anything wrong. He is simply reflecting the background which he brings to school. To change such habits

requires more than just knowledge. Every parent knows that a child who is troubled with thumb-sucking or fingernail-biting is not corrected merely by scolding or by telling him not to do it. Even the kindest and gentlest of parents find it exceedingly difficult to break such habits. These habits are broken by one of two major forces: The creation of an environment in which the habit could not take place, as for example the use of thumb guards, gloves, and so on; or by some kind of social pressure such as the satisfaction which comes from co-operating with others, or the joy of gaining a personal victory. These same forces may be effectively used in the classroom to change undesirable usage habits. It requires the presentation of the desired form and specific practice in its development with unceasing vigilance for any relapses. This is the kind of environment which will change habits. The child must be assisted to discover when he is on the verge of uttering an expression not desired. If he can learn in time to correct himself before he utters the undesirable form, he will quickly assume the new habit. He will even take pride in using the new speech form which the teacher desires. Knowledge of the structure of English may assist in such corrections but almost never provides the motivation for their actual development.

3. All the evidence available shows that formal grammar has little or no effect upon the skills of composition in the elementary grades. Many studies have been carried out to determine the relationship between structural grammar and the writing skills of children. As early as 1923 William Asher conducted such an inquiry into the writing abilities of children in the upper elementary grades and derived this conclusion: "We may, therefore, be justified in the conclusion that time spent upon formal grammar in the elementary school is wasted so far as a majority of students is concerned." [4] Other studies working on this same problem have yielded the same conclusions.

4. Various studies which have been conducted over the years

[4] William Asher, "Does Knowledge of Formal Grammar Function?" School and Society, Vol. 17 (January 27, 1923), pp. 109–111.

indicate that grammatical terminology, when not particularly connected with a skill regularly used by the child, is easily confused and forgotten. All teachers know how difficult it is even after the passage of a short time to have children recall the grammatical terminology which they have learned only a few weeks earlier. After a summer vacation almost all grammar has to be retaught. This is true even in the high school, where it is quite customary for the teacher of sophomore or junior English to begin over again the basic terms of grammar with students who have been away from it for two or three months. With this evidence before us it seems, indeed, unnecessary and perhaps a waste of the student's time to attempt to teach the formal terms of grammar in the elementary grades. To avoid teaching these terms does not mean that the child is unable to learn them. The question is how much effort is required and how valuable is the effort at this point. There is no evidence to show that excellent writing and speaking result, at least through grade six, from teaching the terms of formal grammar. In fact, the reverse seems to be true, that where a great deal of grammar is taught at the expense of practice in writing and speaking, the children make very poor gains in their English expression. It is wasteful of student and teacher time to attempt the mastery of grammatical terms at least until the beginning of the seventh year.

TERMINOLOGY INCIDENTALLY USED

No good teacher would refuse to answer a fair question asked by a pupil. Therefore, if in any of the elementary grades a child asks a specific question which calls for an answer in the form of a term of grammar, the teacher would naturally give that term. It is quite likely, therefore, that such words as *noun*, *verb*, possibly *adjective* and *adverb*, will develop. Surely the word *sentence* will occur frequently in the discussion of the formation of the child's writing. The significant point here is that while these terms may be used incidentally and to answer the questions of students, they do not constitute materials on which he is to be drilled or on which he is to give the answers in the form of identification and definitions.

The English language is in itself an exceedingly interesting study. It is perhaps true that in the past we have devoted too much time in the elementary grades to the purely formal structure of the language and have ignored its interesting byways and highways. Children's attention can be directed to observing the way that language works. They should be asked to test out the effectiveness of certain kinds of phrases in certain kinds of situations. They can be made to be alert to the usage of their parents, to people in their communities, to each other in various situations. They may be interested in trying to judge which of several expressions is both the most effective and the most satisfactory in some situations. Moreover, they can become interested in words. Words have histories. Words have interesting backgrounds. Words have varieties of meanings, some of which will be quite unknown to the children. This kind of material constitutes an introduction to the English language of a nature far more interesting to the elementary school child and far more valuable in developing an attitude on his part of respect for his language than does the structure of formal grammar. Surely there is time enough in the junior high school and senior high school to teach those elements of the structure of his language which he will need for more advanced composition.

REFERENCES

Barrows, Marjory Westcott, *Good English Through Practice* (New York, Henry Holt and Co., 1956).

Kibbe, Delia E., LaBrant, Lou, and Pooley, Robert C., *Handbook of English for Boys and Girls* (Chicago, Scott, Foresman and Co., 1939).

Pooley, Robert C., *Teaching English Usage* (New York, Appleton-Century-Crofts, Inc., 1946).

Curriculum Commission, National Council of Teachers of English, *Language Arts for Today's Children* (New York, Appleton-Century-Crofts, Inc., 1954).

XI

Grammar in the
Junior High School

THE PRECEDING CHAPTER states the point of view that the teaching of structural parts of the English language (parts of speech, subject, verb, object, and so on) may wisely be deferred until the seventh grade. This deferment does not in any way indicate a lessening of attention to learning to use English effectively. On the contrary, the deferment of structural grammar has as one leading reason the release of time for increased practice in speaking and writing. Nor does the deferment of structural grammar indicate any slackening of attention to sound usage and the correction of those errors of usage or bad habits of expression which should receive attention in the elementary school curriculum. The point is made that in the first six grades the child will make greater progress in good English by practicing in speech and writing the desired and approved forms of English than by learning rules, principal parts, and other structural matters. The goal of the grades through six in the language arts should be to encourage in every way the use of language in spoken and written communication, to correct where necessary the misuse of English forms or persistent bad habits, and to pass on to the junior high school children eager to talk and write with improved habits in these skills.

THE POINT OF VIEW

If, then, we accept the deferment of structural grammar to the seventh school year, what shall be the curriculum in grammar of the junior high school? By junior high school is meant grades seven, eight, and nine; in some school systems grades seven and eight will be part of the elementary school system (the upper grades) and grade nine will be the first year of the high school. The curriculum principles and materials offered in this chapter are intended for grades seven, eight, and nine, regardless of the type of school organization. To answer the question briefly, the curriculum in grammar for grades seven and eight will be *the establishment of the structure of the simple sentence, with all the parts of speech related to it,* and in grade nine *the addition of the adverb clause to develop an introduction to the complex sentence.* The remainder of this chapter will discuss the reasons for this limitation of the curriculum, and will develop and illustrate effective classroom methods for the creation of a genuine grammatical understanding.

ROTE LEARNING VS. FUNCTIONAL LEARNING

Seventh-grade pupils of ordinary intelligence and reasonably active memories can learn a large number of grammatical terms and rules. This learning is especially apt to take place if the teacher is pleasant and competent, can secure and hold the attention of the pupils, and can make the presentation of grammatical ideas interesting. Under such circumstances pupils "learn" very well; they can repeat terms and rules when asked to do so, and can pass examinations on such materials. It is this kind of learning that is usually meant when a teacher says, "I have no trouble with grammar; my pupils learn everything in the book." The real question, however, is not whether the pupils can "learn" grammatical materials of this kind in this manner, but whether such learning bears any direct relationship to the purpose for the teaching of grammar, which is primarily to accomplish the writing of better sentences. This goal is achieved only when each grammatical term or rule is derived from, and is immediately associated with, its function in the writing of English sentences. In general the teaching of grammar, and especially the teaching of grammar in the junior high school, lacks this functional relationship and is therefore an exercise of the memory on materials detached from their functional uses, rather than the learning of functional processes.

Using the same methods as are customarily employed in teaching grammar, a seventh-grade teacher could with equal ease have his pupils "learn" the table of chemical elements with their atomic weights, or the bones of the human body, or any other organized table of knowledge. We do not teach these matters in the junior high school because we perceive easily that they are not functionally useful to the pupils. The point of this discussion is that much of the grammar now taught in the seventh and eighth grades, and especially in the manner by which it is taught, is equally nonfunctional, and if learned, is learned by memory only.

CUMULATIVE LEARNING OF GRAMMAR

The terms of grammar may be fairly easily committed to memory, and certain rules to govern specific instances in English usage may be similarly learned. But the concepts of grammar, those understandings which enable one to observe his language scientifically and to make independent judgments in its use, are of a complex nature and require the power to derive generalizations from a large number of particular instances. This power develops with maturity, and to give students such power is a very different matter from having them memorize terms and rules. It requires that our instruction parallel their growth in maturity. Since maturity is another way of saying slowly developing and expanding abilities, it follows that growth in the grasp of grammatical concepts will be slow and gradual, rather than rapid and immediate. In instructional terms, this means that the materials of grammar to be taught must be carefully controlled to remain within the average comprehension level of the pupils, and that a few concepts taught slowly and thoroughly will bring about functional understandings in a way that rapid memorization can never accomplish.

This principle of slowly developing power in grammatical understanding is not very evident in the schools. The vast majority of curriculums and the textbooks of the most popular publishers contain in the book or outline for the seventh grade more grammar than is taught in some college classes: all the parts of speech, all the functions of words in sentences, all types of modification, and all the verbals. This material, supposedly taught in the seventh grade, is repeated in the outlines and books of the eighth grade, the ninth grade, and in each successive grade or book to high school graduation. Under this system very few students really learn grammar, most students have to be retaught annually what they have forgotten from the previous year, and the attitude toward grammar developed by such instruction predisposes students to resist further teaching. Some develop an impregnable immunity to grammar.

To sum the point up quickly: the traditional curriculum in the teaching of grammar has sought to teach too much grammar, too early, too fast. The point of view of this treatment is that grammar can be learned better, retained longer, and more readily applied to the writing of English if it is taught a few concepts at a time, carefully developed, immediately applied to writing, and frequently exercised in useful situations. Such teaching calls for a carefully planned curriculum, a clear understanding of the limits and responsibilities of the teacher of each grade level, and the ability to bring about functional learning rather than rote memory. The following sections will develop the outline of a cumulative curriculum, and will present examples of inductive teaching leading to functional understanding.

A CUMULATIVE PROGRAM IN GRAMMAR

Since the purpose of a cumulative program in grammar is to slow down instruction to the point where students may grasp, understand, and apply usefully the elements they are learning, it is of utmost importance that each term or concept when it is offered be developed, discussed, applied, and practiced until each pupil of normal learning ability has gained both the understanding and the use of the term or concept. An effort has been made in the following outline to present terms and concepts in their probable order of useful learning, the principle being that each new term bears some functional relationship to one or more previous terms and also lays a foundation for the understanding and use of one or more subsequent terms. The teacher should make every effort to awaken in the minds of the pupils these associations and relationships among terms. Memorized definitions of terms should be avoided, for the meaning of each term should gradually evolve from its use in the creating and analysis of English sentences. The functional purpose of recognizing and using each grammatical element should be kept uppermost in the pupils' minds. Testing of the pupils' grasp of the elements should take the form of the construction of sentences to illustrate the use of elements rather than the definition of terms or the marking of parts in someone else's sentences.

A CUMULATIVE PROGRAM FOR THE JUNIOR HIGH SCHOOL

Seventh Grade

Goal for achievement: To recognize and use the structural parts of the simple sentence.

Elements to be learned:
subject
verb
noun
pronoun
adjective
predicate noun
predicate pronoun
predicate adjective
direct object
sentence
simple sentence

Comment: Note that the understanding of the concept of a sentence comes at the end and not at the beginning of this development. This placement is fundamental to the point of view of this chapter. The concept of a sentence is a grammatical concept. The student cannot grasp it until he has had enough experience with the basic elements of a sentence to see what a sentence consists of. Definitions of the sentence based upon ideas or thoughts are for practical purposes worthless; the only functionally useful definition of a sentence must show that the sentence contains meaning and is composed of necessary elements. Such a definition would be worded something like this: A sentence is a meaningful group of words composed of a subject (implied or expressed) and a verb.

When the nature of a sentence is clearly understood, the teacher may then indicate that most of the sentences which students will read or write will be either *statements* (the declarative sentence) or *questions* (the interrogative sentence). Further classification at this point will probably confuse more than it will help.

Eighth Grade

Goals for achievement: To recognize and use the compound subject, verb, and complements of the simple sentence, and to learn the nature and use of the modifiers of the simple sentence.

Elements to be learned:
conjunction
the compound subject
the compound verb
complement
the compound complement
modifier
adverb
the indirect object
phrase
prepositional phrase
Optional for more advanced pupils:
the present participle
participial phrases

Comment: At the conclusion of this year's work, if the material has been slowly and thoroughly presented, with much practice and frequent applications, the normal pupil should possess a working comprehension of the structure and parts of the simple English sentence, and should be able to recognize these parts in sentences, and to construct sentences to illustrate the parts. As will be developed in a following section, he should be having regular practice in the association of this grammatical structure with the sentences in his own compositions.

Toward the end of this year's work the classification of sentences may be expanded by teaching the exclamation (the exclamatory sentence) with particular attention to its structure. The student should see that the verb of such a sentence being addressed to a particular person or persons has a perfectly clear subject, but one which does not need to be expressed. The punctuation of the exclamation should accompany the writing of such sentences.

Ninth Grade

Goals for achievement: The modification of a simple sentence by the use of an adverbial clause. To subordinate a predication by forming an adverbial clause. To recognize and use the complex sentence.

Elements to be learned:
    clause
    adverbial clause
    modification of a verb by a clause
    subordination of one structure to another
    adverb as a subordinating conjunction
    complex
    complex sentence

Comment: This year's work would begin with a thorough review of the elements of the simple sentence, for without the grasp of such elements, modification by clauses can become badly confused. Great emphasis should be put upon the structural similarity between a simple clause and a simple sentence, pointing out that most often the adverbial clause is a simple sentence applied to the particular task of modifying the verb of another sentence. Make clear that a clause is created by its functional use, for without its introductory word it usually cannot be distinguished from a simple sentence. Show that the structural definition of a clause is the same as that of a sentence: a clause must express meaning and it must have a subject and a verb.

The success of this cumulative plan demands the understanding and the co-operative action of all of the teachers within a given school or school system. Each teacher of a certain grade must be perfectly clear on three essential curriculum facts: (1) what grammar the students who come to him are supposed to know; (2) what elements of grammar he is supposed to teach for understanding and use; (3) what elements of grammar he must omit from instruction to keep within his assignment. Only by complete agreement with and adherence to these limits can a cumulative, developmental plan work. Within these limits there will also have to be consideration for the minority of students unable to learn even the basic concepts.

DEDUCTIVE AND INDUCTIVE TEACHING

Traditionally a great deal of grammar has been taught by a deductive approach. In this method a rule or principle is stated first, or a definition given, and when this has been memorized and illustrated, the student proceeds to identify the rule, principle, or the item defined in examples of English writing set before him. To illustrate: students have often begun the study of grammar by learning the definition "A noun is the name of a person, place, or thing." This seems very simple and easy, and a good clear way to teach a simple element of grammar. A few moments' reflection, however, will reveal that what the young student usually learns from such instruction is the words of the definition, but very little of the conceptual meaning underlying the words. Even the concept of a name is not too easy. He can see that *Jim, Alfred, Mrs. Jones,* and *Doctor Smith* are names; that *Rocky Mountains, Mississippi River,* and *Sun Valley* are names; perhaps he can follow to the point of recognizing that *ball, house, paper,* and *lamb chops* are names. But what about *hurry, shout, exasperation, visibility, love,* and *sense?* The concept of name applied to such words is difficult to grasp and is indeed a kind of special fiction requiring a special kind of imagination. Any seventh-grade teacher can cite many instances of otherwise reasonably intelligent pupils who seem utterly incapable of making this abstract leap, and who consequently never seem able to grasp fully what is meant by a noun. The difficulties of understanding are even greater when the rule rests upon a greater number of concepts, all of which must be understood for the rule to function in learning. An apparently simple rule is "An adverb is a word that modifies a verb, adjective, or another adverb." In part this rule is circular, for a student is told that he can learn what an adverb is by observing that it modifies another adverb! But overlooking this logical fallacy for the moment, even so simple a rule as this requires that the pupil have a clear understanding of the concept of modification and the ability to identify all verbs and adjectives. In the rapid manner by which such terms and definitions are generally taught, the student lacks clear understandings of the basic concepts and is consequently often confused and discouraged.

Inductive teaching of grammatical concepts is slower, less precise, and more demanding of patience and careful planning on the part of the teacher than is deductive teaching. But the results are in the long run far more satisfactory, for this type of learning leads to understanding and application much more readily than does the memorization of rules. The simplest definition of inductive teaching in grammar is this: that the student derive his definitions and rules from the observation of what happens when he uses English for communication; in other words, that he learn the general facts by the observation and understanding of a large number of particular instances.

By way of illustration, consider the steps involved in learning in the seventh grade the nature and functions of an adjective. In the cumulative plan of instruction the student has already identified nouns and verbs and is familiar with their uses in elementary sentences. He has also learned the concept of the subject. Have one or more students write at the blackboard several simple sentences such as, "The boys ran"; "The friends met"; "People can sing"; "Birds fly"; and the like. The teacher will now rewrite these sentences above or below the original one in each case as follows: "The happy boys ran"; "The old friends met"; "Some people can sing"; "Most birds fly"; and so on. As the students observe these changes in the sentences, the teacher asks: "What have I done by adding these words? What do you know now that you didn't know before?"

In the discussion aroused by the answers to these questions, lead the students to identify the descriptive or limiting words, and to explain in each instance exactly how the subject word has been influenced by the added word. When the significance of the added words has been fully grasped (and let it be repeated that slow, patient teaching is the clue to successful concept-building), then set the students to writing a number of sentences in which the subject is modified by a single adjective, but without using these terms as yet.

Subsequent lessons will follow a similar procedure to show how a word can describe or limit a noun when the noun is the object of a verb. When the students can clearly and easily distinguish the modifying word from the word modified (in other words, distinguish each adjective from the noun it modifies) in the subject position and in the object position, they are ready to learn and use the name of the kind of word they have identified. From this point on, the word *adjective* will be stressed until the word becomes a familiar one, identified with the function which the student has learned in advance. The principle of teaching is this: that the student, by experience with normal English sentences, learns to recognize a particular use or function. When he can recognize the function in written sentences and can create his own sentences employing the function, he is then ready to learn its name and to relate it to the growing body of grammatical knowledge which he is slowly building. Henceforth, to use the illustration above, the name *adjective* awakens a long line of specific instances from which the term was derived.

To continue: When the adjective as the simple modifier of a single noun is a clear and unmistakable concept, then further experience with the adjective is called for. Two or more adjectives modifying the same noun must be experienced, with the appropriate punctuation as part of the experience; then when the time comes for complements to be taught, the adjective as a predicate adjective must be fully experienced in many different situations in the same patient, thorough way suggested for the simple adjective.

The method of instruction illustrated for the adjective applies to all other concepts of grammar. Each new concept builds upon understandings created for one or more previous concepts; each concept well learned is the foundation for the easier learning of subsequent ones. It is a chain of learning in which there must be no weak links!

The general scheme of concept-teaching as illustrated in the foregoing paragraphs may be summarized in the following steps. These do not constitute a law but a suggested plan of procedure.

STEPS IN CONCEPT BUILDING IN GRAMMAR

1. Have students construct sentences lacking the element to be taught.

2. To these sentences add the new element in such a way as to make very clear what has been added.

3. Lead students to recognize what has happened to the meaning or structure of the sentence as a result of the addition.

4. Have students construct many sentences making use of the new element in its normal applications. This is the point to watch for confusions and to assist the student in correcting them.

5. When the use of the element is familiar, when it can be recognized unmistakably in written sentences, and when the student can create sentences using the element accurately; then teach its name, and give sufficient practice in the use of the element thereafter to attach the name to the function it performs.

6. To test the student's grasp of the concept, call upon him to write sentences employing the named element in the various sentence patterns to which it applies.

GRAMMAR IN COMPOSITION

Two axioms of teaching English underlie the theory and practice of this book. These are:

a. Students learn to write by the actual processes of writing; that is, putting words together for the purposes of communication. No amount of time given to grammar teaching, usage drill, or other instruction in the mechanics of composition will teach the skill of writing.

b. The reason for teaching grammar is to improve written sentence structure. Consequently every portion of grammar instruction must be directly related to the process of writing.

One of the memorable passages in Molière's play *The Amateur Gentleman* is the awesome discovery by the hero that all his life he has been speaking prose. This strikes him as a notable fact and fills him with pride. The ideal in teaching grammar would be to have each student discover that all his life he has been using grammar; that grammar is what results when he arranges words into meaningful groups. This fact should strike him as notable and fill him with pride. With such a view he could appreciate and enjoy grammar, rather than fear and detest it. If grammar is directly related to what the student is doing in his writing, he has an opportunity to develop such a view.

It has been stressed in the method suggestions above that the teaching of new grammatical concepts begin with the students' writing of actual sentences and that the new element illustrate its purpose and function in what it does to those sentences. Each concept, then, becomes a new block of material toward the writing of better sentences, or of writing sentences which say better than before exactly what the student wants to say. Grammar in this view is a technique toward the improvement of a vitally important art, so that its teaching should always stress what it does rather than what it is. Grammar is the doorway to better composition.

But composition, too, can play its part in teaching grammar. The interrelationship can be made profitable to the student. The review of any grammatical concept previously taught can best be conducted by setting the student to discover how he has employed the particular element in some recent writing. To illustrate: Suppose that the class has written an exercise in composition of one or more paragraphs on a subject of interest to the members. These compositions may have been read aloud for mutual enjoyment and helpful criticism. Suppose also that the concept of the adverb has been previously taught in the manner suggested above. At a suitable time, distribute the composition papers to their authors, setting them the problem to discover and list on a separate sheet each adverb which they find in the composition. When the adverbs are listed, have them return to their papers to discover and note how each adverb was used. Which ones directly modified verbs? Which ones modified adjectives? Did any modify another adverb? The list, when finished, should contain all the adverbs in the composition, with a note after each as to how it was used.

To strengthen the review, the teacher may at this or another class period have the students exchange papers to check the accuracy of the exercise. Have any adverbs in the composition not been recognized? Is any word incorrectly identified as an adverb? Is the use of each adverb correctly described? Every difference of opinion should be called to the teacher's attention, who may settle the matter by discussion with the students involved, or may use the issue to clear up possible misunderstandings by a blackboard demonstration of the problem. What is educationally important here is that the grammar is the student's own; he used the adverb for a purpose, and if he used it incorrectly, or failed to identify its use, the material is his own, and the correction applies to his own writing. The situation is a real one for him, and the application to his own work may clear up a final confusion in his mind.

CLASSROOM TIME FOR GRAMMAR

Much of the criticism of the teaching of grammar which has led in some instances to its curtailment or even abandonment is not directed so much at the grammar itself as the disproportionate amount of time given to it, or the wasteful use of such time. Grammar is, after all, the means toward the attainment of desirable skills; to let it take the place of the practice in such skills is a misuse of grammar. It is proper here to consider just what time, in what proportion, should be allocated to the teaching of grammar.

In the typical junior high school program of studies, five class periods of from 45 to 60 minutes each are given to the teaching of English each week. There are wide variations from this norm, and there are certain core or integrated programs in which the exercise of certain skills pertaining to English is performed in other subject-matter contexts, such as the social studies. But generally speaking, the junior high school English teacher has something less than five hours a week to give to all the various skills and activities which are classified as English, or the language arts. These constitute three major divisions: (1) the writing skills, including grammar, usage, mechanics (such as punctuation and capitalization), and composition in all its forms, including letter-writing; (2) the reading skills, including the mechanics of reading, the improvement of speed and comprehension, the improvement of reading for factual information, and the enjoyment and appreciation of fine literature; (3) the speaking-listening skills, including voice training, the development of confidence and skill in speaking, the conduct of public meetings, and all the listening skills related to the classroom, to the radio, and to television. No one has ever accused a language arts teacher of not having enough to do!

In the light of so inclusive an obligation to the curriculum and to the students, to give two or more hours a week to instruction in grammar is obviously a disproportionate allowance of time. The scheme of instruction advocated in this chapter and in the book as a whole is that a cumulative program of grammar learning can save time and release time for other more important activities. While no arbitrary time can be set for the teaching of grammar, the reduction of the number of specific elements to be taught in any given school year should certainly assure more time for those that are taught, and time saved from those that are not taught. In grades seven and eight, in a five-hour-a-week program, not more than one hour total in the week should be given to grammar as it is described in this book. Moreover, this hour is preferably not to be used as one solid period, but to be spaced into two halves or three thirds in the program of the week. Concentrated teaching in short periods spaced by short intervals will in most cases produce the most satisfactory results. In the ninth grade, when the students have come up through the cumulative program of grammar, even less time per week need be taken; as a suggestion, the time for grammar might average forty minutes per week.

With shortened allocations of time to grammar, it is essential that the time be most effectively used. Here is an example of time poorly used. An eighth-grade teacher, to review the ability to recognize subjects and verbs in simple sentences, wrote thirty-two sentences on the blackboard. When the students came into the room, she distributed paper with the direction that each student was to copy all the sentences, and to underline each subject with a single line, and each verb with a double line. This exercise took almost the entire hour for the students to write, and left little time for correction or discussion. Moreover, for three-fourths of the students it was a waste of time, for they could already perform the skill and needed no practice in it.

In very much less time the teacher could have sent a portion of the class to the blackboard and have distributed paper to the others at their seats. Her assignment then would be: write three simple sentences of your own, with such modifiers as you wish, and indicate the subject of each sentence by drawing a single line under it; the verb of each sentence by two lines under it. Not much more than five minutes would be required for the writing, leaving fifteen minutes of a twenty-minute period for corrections, explanations, and discussion. Moreover, the teacher would quickly gain an inventory of those in the class who were adequate in the knowledge of subjects and verbs, and could list for additional assistance at another time those who needed more active review. The competent members of the class would not need a review of this particular skill for some time. Their time could be released for other learnings until such time as a new review or a new concept in grammar is to be presented.

SUMMARY

The teaching of grammar in the junior high school should be characterized by (1) a limited number of new concepts to be introduced in each of the three years; (2) the teaching of these concepts in a slow, clear manner to develop understanding and use of the concepts; (3) the application of each new concept to the actual writing of the student, both by having him consciously use the element in his own writing, and by analyzing his writing to discover how he has used the element; and (4) the efficient use of time to avoid wasteful procedures, and to separate the competent students from those who need additional instruction and drill. The time saved by such procedures can profitably be used in the practice of writing.

REFERENCES

Curriculum Commission, National Council of Teachers of English, *Language Arts for Today's Children* (New York, Appleton-Century-Crofts, Inc., 1954).

Curriculum Commission, National Council of Teachers of English, *The English Language Arts in the Secondary School* (New York, Appleton-Century-Crofts, Inc., 1956).

Hook, J. N. *The Teaching of High School English* (New York, The Ronald Press, 1950).

Pooley, Robert C., *Teaching English Usage* (New York, Appleton-Century-Crofts, Inc., 1946).

XII

Grammar in the Senior High School

THE SCHEME OF GRAMMAR INSTRUCTION set forth in this book relies upon a continuity of program in content and methods such as is found in the more highly integrated school systems. Where such integration does not exist, as for example in a village or city high school which draws its students from a large number of surrounding schools under separate administrations, the obvious values of a cumulative, progressive plan of grammar instruction may provide the foundation for some co-operative curriculum work, leading to a better understanding of the total English program among the various schools of the area or community.

TRANSITION FROM THE JUNIOR HIGH SCHOOL

The principal curriculum ideas developed in Chapters X and XI include: (1) that formal instruction in the structure of English may be wisely postponed through the sixth grade, but that great emphasis be laid upon the active use of English in speech and writing to develop a readiness to speak and write; (2) that instruction in the structure of English begin in the seventh grade, but be confined to a few fundamentals slowly and thoroughly taught; and (3) that each grade thereafter maintain the concepts taught in previous grades, and add in the same careful manner the new concepts assigned to it in the cumulative plan. This chapter picks up the program at the senior high school level and continues the

146

cumulative growth program through the twelfth grade to the point of high school graduation. In the total plan, proper recognition is made of the fact that many high school students end their formal instruction in English at the close of the eleventh grade; the twelfth-grade program, therefore, is presented as an elective optional course, though it is one which might profitably be taken by the great majority of high school students.

The term *senior high school* is used in this chapter to designate grades ten, eleven, and twelve. Many senior high schools include the ninth grade. In such schools the program of grammar instruction as outlined in this book would begin with the program for grade nine as presented on pages 134 to 137 in Chapter XI. Fundamental to the total plan is the understanding and acceptance by each teacher of the specific assignment of grammatical materials made to his particular grade or grades. He must expect of incoming students no more knowledge or skill in grammatical elements than the outline has provided for the previous grades. In turn, he must limit his instruction to the specific concepts and skills assigned to the grade he is teaching, with the intention of sending his students on to the next teacher competent in the application of the concepts it was his duty to teach. The more closely these two principles are followed by all the teachers in a school system or co-operative school area, the more chance there is of a satisfactory outcome in the use of grammar by students for improved sentence skills. That the total plan may be more clearly seen, the reader who has not yet read Chapter XI is urged to do so before studying the grammar program presented below for the senior high school.

GRAMMAR IN THE SENIOR HIGH SCHOOL

Earlier schemes for the teaching of English grammar tended to place the burden of the instruction into the upper elementary grades and grades seven and eight of the junior high school level, with review and practice assigned to grades nine and beyond. One reason for this early placement of content was the theory that in order to begin Latin or a modern foreign language in the ninth grade, a student should be instructed in all the elements of English grammar in advance. There are three basic reasons why this early placement of grammar should give way to a more widely distributed assignment of instruction. In the first place it must be remembered that the concepts of grammar are mature concepts, calling for a stage of mental growth at which generalizations may be formed by the observation and analysis of a large number of specific instances. Very few children of eleven and twelve years of age have this power to any high degree, and hence have "learned" grammar by memorization of words rather than by understanding concepts. In the second place, modern teachers of Latin and foreign languages recognize the truth that the grammar of every language is necessarily different from the grammar of every other, and that the grammatical concepts of any particular language are best learned in the context of that language. [1] Consequently the demand for the whole of English grammar prior to the ninth year by teachers of foreign languages is dying out. Third, and most telling, the scheme of early grammar teaching simply has not worked. Students may memorize terms and rules, but these, having no real basis in their understandings, do not function in their use of English and are quickly forgotten. Our schools are filled today with students who have been exposed to two or three years of grammar instruction in the junior high school, yet reveal almost complete ignorance of the elements of the simple sentence. Obviously something is wrong with the content, the grade placement, or the method, or some combination of the three, to produce so unsatisfactory results.

The scheme of slowly developing concepts presented by this book will assign a considerable body of new material to teach in grades ten and eleven. The student who has completed the ninth grade of this plan should know the structure of the simple sentence with its modifiers, and should recognize and use adverbial clauses as modifiers. The tenth-grade teacher must expect no more

[1] See Walter V. Kaulfers, *Four Studies in Grammar* (Stanford, Calif., Stanford Bookstore, 1945).

than these concepts; if they have been effectively taught, a short review in the application of these learnings to sentence construction should provide the foundation for the new concepts of the tenth grade. These concepts, so important to the composition skills needed by the student, come at a time when his expanding powers of written composition make immediately useful to him the grammatical concepts and devices of the grammar program.

A CUMULATIVE PROGRAM FOR
THE SENIOR HIGH SCHOOL
Tenth Grade

Goals for achievement: The modification of a simple sentence by the use of an adjective clause. To subordinate a predication by forming an adjective clause. To use a noun clause as subject or object of an element in a main clause or principal sentence. To subordinate a predication by forming a noun clause. To practice subordination by the use of participial phrases and appositional phrases.

Elements to be learned:
adjective clause
modification of a noun by a clause
relative pronoun
antecedent
restrictive clause
nonrestrictive clause
punctuation of nonrestrictive clauses
noun clause
clause as subject
clause as object of a verb
clause as predicate complement
clause as object of a preposition
present participle
past participle
perfect participle
participial phrase
appositive
apposition
appositional phrase
modification by apposition

Notes for teaching. The grammar program of the tenth grade might very well begin after the students have written the first composition. When the papers have been returned, the students could be given the assignment to locate the first simple sentence in each composition, to copy the sentence out, and to indicate its structure, either by the use of a diagram or by the marking of the main elements and the modifiers. If some of the exercises are done at the blackboard while the remainder are inspected by the teacher, it should be fairly easy to locate the students for whom a more thoroughgoing review would be advisable. At this time, or at a suitable time thereafter, a review session on the simple sentence should be planned for those students who need the work. Competent students can be assigned an exercise in reading or writing while the practice session is in progress. One or more such sessions should bring the great majority of the class to a point where the structure of the simple sentence is a usable reality. The next step in the grammar program might be to set the students to discover adverbial clauses in their own writing, using the same procedures as above until the great majority of the students show command of the structure of the complex sentence using an adverbial clause.

Probably the easiest way to begin the study of the adjective clause is to list on the blackboard the five common relative pronouns, *who, whom, whose, which*, and *that*. Since one of these words will introduce nearly every adjective clause the student will read or write, they serve as useful guides to the recognition of the adjective clause. (The use of *that* with the noun clause will be discussed later.) In a parallel column on the blackboard write a number of subjects with articles or adjectives, for example, *two men, the sisters, a car, an arctic explorer, some problems*, asking students to combine the subjects with relative pronouns to form incomplete statements such as "Two men whose shoes were covered with snow"; "The sisters that run the bakery shop," and so on until a considerable number of such combinations has been used. In each instance the teacher should point out how the words following the relative pronoun describe or limit the subject in the same manner as a simple adjective. When these combinations and their adjective quality have been fully discussed and practiced, the students can build sentences by adding predicates to the incompleted statements. Besides teaching the use of the adjective clause, this exercise tends to strengthen the recognition of the whole sentence by emphasizing the incompleteness of the expression without an adequate predicate.

The next stage is to lead students to write a considerable number of sentences employing the adjective clause, first in separate form, and then in context. A composition might follow of a type in which the adjective clause would be normally used.

For an association with usage point out to students what constructions in popular speech are replaced by the adjective clause in writing and formal speech. In general it will be the "and he, and she, and it" constructions that are replaced. Common to student speech is the construction, "My mother has a friend and she told me about living in California." The written equivalent uses the adjective clause: "My mother has a friend *who* told me about living in California." Common in speech also is the type of adjective clause following an object or a predicate noun which is used without a relative pronoun. Example, "John is the boy (that) I like best"; "That's the sled I want for Christmas." This construction is perfectly correct and may be used in writing, though in a more formal style the tendency is to include the relative pronoun. ²

As has been fully developed in Chapter XI, the kind of concept teaching outlined here calls for slow and patient repetition, with frequent practice in short periods at short intervals. The gradual familiarity with the complex sentence, reinforced with constant practice in short written passages, will bring about great improvement in sentence structure in composition, which is the purpose for which grammar is taught. It is possible, therefore, that if the course

² Some curious student may enjoy analyzing the word *that* as it is used in this sentence: "That that that that that modifies is a relative pronoun."

of study provides for grammar and composition throughout the tenth year, the adjective clause will occupy the grammar time of the first semester, together with the complex sentence employing adjective and adverbial clauses. In any event, the noun clause should not be scheduled for instruction until the adjective clause has been absorbed by the students to the point of easy and frequent use.

The noun clause, although it is often described as a dependent clause, bears a different relationship to the syntax of the sentence in which it occurs from that of the adverbial and adjectival clause. The noun clause is rarely a modifier; it is usually the expansion of a main element of the sentence, such as the subject or the object. Consequently, it is best introduced as the direct object of such verbs as *learned, discovered, said, planned*, and similar verbs. Instruction might begin with a list at the blackboard like this:

John learned
The girls discovered
Mother said
The club planned
   etc.

The task set the class is to add a *clause* after each of these incomplete statements which will answer the question "what?" for each verb. Students should find little difficulty in completing the statements, but the teacher will have to watch for infinitive phrases mistakenly offered as clauses. This exercise should be repeated often enough, with new sentences, of course, that each student can make the association between the clause that completes the sentence and the object that completes the verb. When this association is accomplished, the main use and the basic concept of the noun clause are established.

The noun clause as subject is most easily introduced by the use of clauses beginning with *how, where, what*, and *that*. For example:

how we would spend the summer
where Tom lived as a child
what we should do next
that the road was blocked

These and similar clauses can be looked at by the students as units of idea waiting to be completed by an appropriate predicate. They will find it interesting to add the variety of predicates which can complete such preliminary predications. The essential point is to concentrate the students' attention upon the unity of the initial clause, letting them prove to themselves that the clause is a whole unit acting as subject, and that no part of the clause by itself can be the subject of the main verb. This awareness can be strengthened by the use of diagrams to show visually how the subject unit is related to the predicate of the main clause.

It is at this point that the use of *that* to introduce a noun clause as compared with *that* to introduce an adjective clause is best discussed. Emphasize the need to examine closely any clause beginning with *that;* to be careful not to jump to a conclusion; to test the *that* for its use in the clause and its relationship to the remainder of the sentence. There is no need for over-refinement on this point, but only to caution the students about the possible confusion in clauses beginning with *that.*

The student has learned the noun clause as a unit which takes the place of a noun; he can learn next that an appositive word or phrase is a unit which stands beside a noun. The appositive is a construction best learned by observation before the name is applied (see pages 137 to 140 in Chapter XI). Begin instruction with a list of typical appositions, such as:

John, my younger brother,
Tom Jones, the quarterback,
My father's friend, that radio announcer,
Judy Miggs, a promising young actress,
    etc.

Let the students provide appropriate predicates for such sentences and, after sufficient practice, let them create whole sentences using appositives in the subject position and in the object position. Follow this exercise with the writing of a composition in which a reasonable number of appositive phrases may appear.

The next step is to show how the appositive can reduce predication; that is, take the place of a clause. Present a blackboard list such as:

who is our neighbor
who was a traveler
which is a cereal
that is not needed at present

Have the students identify these first as adjective clauses. Then let them build sentences incorporating these clauses. Next, ask them to strike out the subject and verb of each adjective clause. What is left? Let them tell you. Now have them construct a number of sentences, some of which use the adjective clause, and some the parallel appositive. Lead them to form an opinion as to the use of the appositive, what is gained by it, and when it is better to use the adjective clause. Since these decisions are made in context for purely subjective reasons, respect reasonable opinions. But let them see, by illustrations supplied by the teacher, that in long constructions employing a number of clauses, the reduction of one or more predications by the use of apposition is a net gain in the compactness of the sentence.

Review the present participle as a tool in the reduction of a clause to a phrase. Then show how the past participle often functions in a manner very similar to apposition in the saving of words, as in such constructions as: "The lamp, lighted an hour earlier" (which had been lighted an hour earlier); "The belated travelers, now arrived" (who had now arrived); and many others. The ability to use the two constructions, the apposition and the past participle phrase, will lend clarity and brevity to students' sentence structures not otherwise attained. Give them plenty of practice in these constructions in actual compositions.

Calling attention to the punctuation of the appositive phrase and the past participle phrase as inserted elements interrupting the movement of the sentence provides a very good introduction to the troublesome nonrestrictive adjective clause. There is no grammatical problem; it is simply one of conventional punctuation of the nonrestrictive clause. The restrictive adjective clause is essential to the identification of the word it modifies. Without the clause, the noun is insufficiently identified, as in such examples as: "The boy who just came in"; "That tree which leans over the fence"; "The store that had a fire last week"; and so on. In these cases it can be shown that without the clause the noun is unidentified; consequently, the clause does not interrupt the flow and needs no punctuation to set it off from the remainder of the sentence.

The nonrestrictive clause, on the other hand, is a gratuitous addition to a noun already identified, as for example: "Dr. Leonard Woods, who came to New York as a child, told of his early days . . ."; "Miss Marie Scott, who was my kindergarten teacher, met me . . ."; "The abandoned farmhouse near the top of the hill, which for so many years was an eyesore, was finally blown over. . . ." Because the nonrestrictive clause adds a supplementary piece of information, it is felt to be an interruption to the flow between subject and verb, and is consequently set off in commas. In this pattern of punctuation it is parallel with other supplementary interrupters, such as the apposition, the adjective phrase, some adverb phrases, and other gratuitous insertions between the subject and the predicate.

Eleventh Grade

Goals for achievement: The effective use of verbals; that is, participles, gerunds, and infinitives for sentence variety. Variety in the use of basic sentence structures: the simple sentence, the simple sentence with verbal phrases, the complex sentence, the compound sentence, and the compound-complex sentence. Use of the semicolon sentence. Effective placement of modifying words and phrases. Varieties of sentence patterns: regular, inverted, and elliptical, together with variety in sentence length.

Elements to be learned: verbal (sometimes called verbid)
                       gerund
                       infinitive
                       gerund phrase
                       infinitive phrase
                       verbals as subjects, objects, and complements
                       verbals as modifiers
                       compound-complex sentence
                       semicolon sentence
                       word order
                       position of modifiers

Notes for teaching. The eleventh year is the capstone year of instruction in the cumulative plan of grammar teaching offered by this book. Since it is the final year of English instruction for a great many students, even of many who go on to college, there is need to present in this year the elements of English sentence structure which have so far been omitted, or only lightly touched upon. Since the principal purpose of grammar study is the improvement of written sentences, it is assumed that the major emphasis of this year will be upon composition. Writing will provide the opportunity to apply the goals of achievement for this year's work toward an increasing command of all the patterns of sentence structure which the flexibility of modern English will offer him.

The emphasis of the tenth-year grammar program was upon the clause as a modifier and a sentence element, providing variety of expression and the reduction of independent predications. Toward the end of the tenth year the apposition was studied as a particular kind of phrase modifier which could take the place of an adjective clause and thus further reduce predication.

The verbals, which make up the chief study of the eleventh year in grammar, are best approached as words forming phrases for the efficient introduction of ideas into sentences. Since the present and past participle are already known as single words and phrase-forming words, the study of verbals appropriately begins with a review of the uses of the present and past participles. The perfect participle may be added at this point. The structural emphasis to develop in this review is the *adjective* quality of the uses of the participles, both as single-word modifiers, and as words forming phrases. When the participles have been used in all their various forms and combinations to produce adjective modifications, continue the review to include adjective phrases formed with prepositions.

The infinitive is best introduced as a noun with the particular quality of being able to name an action and yet serve as the subject or object of another verb. Begin with subject situations, such as:

> to dance
> to swim
> to drive a car
> to approach the question intelligently
>   etc.

Lead students to form complete statements with simple infinitives and then with infinitive phrases as the subjects. To demonstrate the object uses of the infinitive, begin with short subject-verb combinations such as:

> Fred learned
> No student offered
> The boat began
> The firemen wanted

to which the students are to add objects beginning with an infinitive.

When the noun uses of the infinitive and infinitive phrase as subject and object have been well developed, the use of the infinitive as adverb should come next. In each case when an infinitive was object of the verb, it answered the question "what?" with regard to that verb. Point out how the infinitive as adverb answers the question "why?" for the verb to which it is related. Illustrate with sentence beginnings such as:

> The girls came (why)
> The teacher repeated the question (why)
> Several more persons were invited (why)

and assist students to complete with infinitive phrases of cause or reason. The somewhat rare use of the infinitive as adjective can be demonstrated without much teaching effort. When an infinitive is needed as an adjective, the speaker or writer uses it so naturally; but the occasions for its need are few. Consequently no great fuss should be made about learning it, or identifying it. The usual situations are like these:

> Boats *to rent at this time of year* are dirty and water-soaked.
> The agent looked about eagerly for a house *to sell to his client*.
> The exercise *to rewrite* is on page six.

Just as with the participle its adjective quality must be stressed, so with the gerund its *noun* quality must be stressed. Indeed, it is best called a *verbal noun*. By itself the verbal noun is grammatically like any other noun: *swimming, jumping, driving, eating, teaching*, all are names of activities just like tennis, baseball, or bridge. But the verbal noun has an added usefulness in being able to convey the quality of its action to an object while still remaining a noun. In this fashion it becomes a convenient device for forming noun phrases which act like all nouns in being subjects of verbs, objects of verbs, and objects of prepositions. In the art of writing varied and interesting sentences, the gerund and its phrase is just one more device for the practical needs of a writer.

Since the gerund and gerund phrase parallel the infinitive and the infinitive phrase in their subject and object uses, the same techniques as suggested above for the infinitive would be used for the gerund. One use of the gerund is as the object of a preposition, a construction for introducing the concept of action into a modifier. Illustrate it with such sentences as:

> The room *for making chemical experiments* is called a laboratory.
> The child was prevented *from injuring himself*.
> *By taking great pains* the exercise can be done neatly.
> *Unlike gathering mushrooms*, the picking of berries is easy.

In these and similar illustrations point out how the gerund phrase acts exactly like a noun in following the preposition, yet takes on the vigor of a verb in being able to name an action which can take its own object. In certain situations the gerund can be an adverb. It is not necessary to teach or test these uses, but they may be pointed out. Just as in the sentence "The boy went home," the word *home* is an adverb, so in the sentence "The boy went *hunting*," the gerund is an adverb.

In their writing, eleventh-grade students should be striving to produce longer sentence structures of properly related parts. As an aid to this goal, the compound-complex sentence may be reviewed and practiced. Make sure that students are clear about the structure of the compound sentence. After a number of plain compound sentences have been written and analyzed, set the assignment of adding a dependent element to one part of the compound sentence. When this step has become clear and easy, have the students make compound sentences with both parts modified by dependent clauses. The purpose, of course, is not to do tricks of grammar but to see how more material (thought-content) can be added to the structure of a single sentence. This and similar exercises should be followed as early as possible with paragraph or theme writing in which the sentence structures just studied can be applied to practical communication.

Although students will long since have been using the semicolon sentence (the compound sentence with the two parts separated by a semicolon), this will be a good time to review its structure and to renew in the minds of students the convention of written English that predications are *separated*. This rule might be given here as an aid to what is called "sentence-sense." "Every predication is *separated* from every other predication by: a period; a semicolon; a conjunction." Like all language rules, this has its exceptions (for example, certain noun clauses like "He said he was hungry"), but for most situations it is an aid to students to avoid the comma fault of writing: "We went to New York last summer, we saw the Yankees play a double-header game." In certain college composition courses the ability of a student to write clean semicolon sentences is taken to be a sign of writing maturity.

The close of the eleventh year of grammatical instruction should be the review of all basic sentence structures in written composition, with commendation for students who can achieve well-constructed paragraphs of varied patterns of sentences.

Twelfth Grade

Goals for achievement: The ability to write, recognize, and name the common structures of the English sentence: the simple sentence, the compound sentence, the complex sentence, and their combinations. The ability to create a pleasing style by the use of varied sentence length and by the effective employment of phrases of all types. To recognize the effectiveness of varied sentence patterns created by the placement of modifiers.

Elements to be learned: word order (syntax)
deferred subjects
cognate objects
voice, active and passive
the object with a passive verb

Notes for teaching. As the whole structure of the English sentence in its ordinary uses has been presented earlier, there is little new material for this year of English instruction in grammar. However, it is an important year in growth and maturity in writing skills, in which grammar will play an important part. The emphasis will be upon continued advance in the utilization of all the varieties in pattern of sentence structure which have been earlier taught.

Perhaps the most useful technique for promoting skills in sentence variety is to demonstrate the many ways in which an English sentence may begin. The list below names the nature of the structure and illustrates it.

Ways to Begin English Sentences

1. Subject alone	John drove his car.
2. Article + subject	The children ran away.
3. Adjective + subject	Large trees require much water.
4. Adverb before subject	Quickly the windows were closed.
5. Prepositional phrase first	
As adjective	From my class, only two boys were chosen to attend the meeting.
As adverb	From the edge of the woods we could see the calm and peaceful lake.
6. Participial phrase first	
Present participle	Taking a short-cut, the boy soon reached the fair-grounds.
Past participle	His work completed, the janitor locked the doors and left.
Perfect participle	Having examined all the maps, I chose a route which avoided the large cities.
7. Infinitive as subject	To win was his first consideration.
	To overcome all obstacles to his final success consumed the leader's time and attention.
8. Gerund as subject	Swimming is great fun.
	Repairing tires for cars and trucks kept Tom busy through most of the year.
9. Postponed subjects	There are *six rules* in that club.
	There was no *end* to his troubles.
	It is certain *that he will win.*
10. Adverbial clause first	When the train came in, I searched for my brother.
11. Noun clause first	How he could avoid doing his chores puzzled the lazy boy.
	That no one knew the answer was clear.
12. Verb first ⎡ To be used	⎤ Arrived at last the long awaited day!
only for great	
13. Object first ⎣ emphasis!	⎦ A fresh start, the student decided he must have.

14. Conjunction first	But the last was best of all!
15. Expletive first	Well, that is finally done.
	Alas, we have no meat for dinner.

In the composition program of the senior year, short reviews of these many constructions can be interspersed with the view of providing the students with specific techniques for the writing of interesting sentences and the development of an effective style. From time to time, students under the direction of the teacher should analyze the sentence structure of a paragraph or two from a current composition, following a pattern of analysis something like this:

a. Count the number of simple sentences, complex sentences, compound sentences, and combinations. Is there an appropriate variety? What further combinations might be used to improve the relationships of ideas, and reduce unnecessary predication?

b. What variety occurs in the beginnings of the sentences? Is the pattern too regular? What changes in the position of modifiers or in the employment of beginning phrases might improve the structure of the paragraph as a whole?

c. Read the paragraph aloud or to yourself. Does it read smoothly? Does the position of any element in any of the sentences produce an awkwardness in reading or in the flow of ideas? If so, what changes in structure might improve this spot?

It is understood that not every student will be able to make use of the full implications of this analysis; even skilled adults vary in their ability to revise English prose to the point of the most effective syntax for the expression of any particular line of thought. Nevertheless, the students who reach the senior year of high school English, and especially those who have come through a developmental plan of practical grammar, can profitably relate grammatical structure to the attainment of more satisfactory writing, and will find simultaneously more sense to the grammar and specific techniques for improving writing. This achievement, even though it will vary in degree for different students, is the real end and purpose of grammar teaching.

Irregular Syntax

As has been developed in Chapter VII, the sentence structure of English prose is normally quite regular, the pattern of subject-verb-complement predominating. Students will note in their reading, variations from this pattern, and will, of course, in their own speech unconsciously produce inversions as the occasion demands. These inversions can properly become the subject of more conscious recognition in the senior year.

The principal inversions of normal sentence pattern are, in approximately the order of their frequency of occurrence:

a.	The interrogative sentence	Do *you* like this kind of pie?
b.	The postponed subject	It is true *that he can swim a mile.*
		There will be *five men* at the party.
c.	Verb first in a statement	After the long night came *the dawn* at last.
d.	Object first in a statement	Shrieks *he* made, till the ears ached.

An interesting discussion can be held on the effects produced by these inversions. Point out that (*a*) is a conventional signal which says, "This is not a statement but a question." Example (*b*) is an idiomatic device to allow the subject to receive a kind of emphasis of position by following the verb. Examples (*c*) and (*d*) are emergency devices: too striking for regular prose, they are reserved for positions of great emphasis in which the action, or the object of the action, is to be made especially prominent.

Other unusual, but fairly frequently used constructions are:

a.	the cognate object	The coach made John *captain.*
b.	the retained object	Mary was given a *necklace.*

This latter construction offers a good introduction to the distinction between the active and the passive voice. The actual signification of this sentence is "To Mary a necklace was given," in which the subject is *necklace* and the verb is in the passive form. However, our sense of the regular pattern of English makes us feel that *Mary* is the subject, and that *necklace* is the object, even though the verb is passive in form.

In the active voice the subject is the "doer" of an action, and the object is the "receiver" of the action. In the passive voice, the object of the active verb becomes the subject of the passive verb, and the former subject, if it appears, becomes an adverbial modifier. Note these examples:

Active voice	*Passive voice*
Professor Smith gave the lecture.	The lecture was given by Professor Smith.
John drove the car.	The car was driven by John.
The senior class gave a party, and invited all the juniors to come and bring their dates.	A party was given by the senior class, and the juniors were invited to come and bring their dates.

The active voice is generally preferable for narrative and exposition because it carries a quality of movement and immediacy which is lacking in the passive voice. The passive voice, however, has a particular quality of presenting the feeling of an action acomplished, of something completed in the past. It is therefore very useful in summarizing and in subordinating past actions in a passage which leads into present action.

Example of desirable use of the passive voice: "The day was decided upon, the list of guests was drawn up, and the invitations were prepared and placed in the mail. Mary breathed a sigh of relief and relaxed to await the party."

Example of less desirable use of the passive voice: "The ball was hit by the second-baseman, the bat was dropped, and first base was reached. The decision was made, however, that the ball was received by the first-baseman before the bag was touched by the runner." Because this passage describes a vigorous series of actions, its ideas are more effectively presented in the active voice. "The second-baseman hit the ball, dropped the bat, and reached first base. The umpire decided, however, that the first-baseman had the ball before the runner hit the sack."

Some practice in writing short paragraphs in the active voice and the passive voice will give students a feeling for the more appropriate construction for the presentation of certain kinds of ideas.

The Senior Grammar Review

Because a number of the seniors who elect the fourth year of English in high school expect to enter college, and because a number of colleges administer tests which call for familiarity with the terms of grammar, it is advisable to conduct a review of the basic terms of grammar in the final weeks of the senior year. For students who have come through a developmental plan of grammatical knowledge such as is outlined in this book the review in most cases can be fairly rapid. These students will need to refresh their understandings of such terms as *subject, predicate, direct object, predicate noun,* and so on, together with a review of the parts of speech.

As has been suggested earlier, this kind of review should be conducted with the greatest regard for the efficient use of the time. Simple diagnostic tests of familiarity with grammatical terms can be constructed by the teacher (see Chapter XIV for examples), administered to the class, and quickly scored. The results of such testing should reveal what matters require further instruction, and what students need particular help. Competent students should be excused from further review. Those who need a little extra practice should receive drills and a second test to permit them to demonstrate competence. The smaller number who need more thorough work can be separated from the class for short periods at frequent intervals for practice and instruction.

Workbooks in the Senior High School

The great majority of workbooks published for the use of high school teachers do not contain grammar of the kind discussed in this book. For the most part they consist of exercises in the correction of usage, some of it reasonably useful, some of it at variance with the actual usage of current English. All the exercises, however, are artificial in the sense that they are detached from the actual writing and speaking of the student. Because they have very little to offer on the structure of English, and because they occupy a great deal of time in the correcting of errors which often are not related to the students' actual needs, it is fair to say that the use of workbooks will not sucessfully advance the kind of growth in knowledge of English and power to write effectively for which this program stands.

REFERENCES

Kaulfers, Walter V., *Four Studies in Grammar* (Stanford University, Cal., Stanford Bookstore, 1945).

Pooley, Robert C., *Teaching English Usage* (New York, Appleton-Century-Crofts, Inc., 1946).

Curriculum Commission, National Council of Teachers of English, *The English Language Arts in the Secondary School* (New York, Appleton-Century-Crofts, Inc., 1956).

XIII

Grammar in College Composition

ENGLISH GRAMMAR is customarily studied or utilized at various points or levels in the college program of studies in English. Grammar appears in the basic composition courses, in upper level composition, in courses on the teaching of English, in courses on the history and development of the English language, in seminars at the graduate level on the development of English, or in courses devoted to historical grammar itself. The discussion of grammar in college courses in this chapter will be confined to the first area only: the use of grammar in the basic composition courses. Even here there is considerable variety in the teaching of grammar, because of differences of point of view of the nature and use of grammar in composition, differences of quantity of the grammatical elements considered important, and differences of method in the actual instruction. This chapter can by no means explore all these variations, but will treat of grammar from what appear to be three fairly distinctive points of view.

APPROACHES TO GRAMMAR IN
BASIC COMPOSITION

There seems to be almost universal agreement that some kind of grammar is an essential part of the basic composition course at the college level. Textbooks designed for such courses and outlines of courses invariably contain units or sections on the teaching of grammar. So far as there can be any official pronouncement in such a matter, it would seem to be contained in the workshop reports of the Conference on College Composition and Communication, an organization within the National Council of Teachers of English devoted to all aspects of the teaching of composition. It is familiarly known as CCCC and will be so called hereafter in this chapter. Ever since its founding in 1949–50, the CCCC has at its annual convention dealt with the subject of grammar in composition. Although a minority of the membership of this society has argued that grammar can be dispensed with if a thorough study of the spoken language and the written language is substituted for grammar, this attitude is in a sense a clash of terminology, for most students of language would agree that a thorough study of the spoken and written aspects of a language would be dealing with grammar, even if under some other name. At any rate, the place of grammar in basic composition has been recognized by its having a regular and important place in the deliberations of the CCCC.[1]

In the meetings of the CCCC in 1950 and 1951 there were large workshops assigned to the consideration of grammar in composition. In total, these groups numbered over sixty persons representing at least fifty colleges and universities of the United States. The workshop group of 1950 made these specific recommendations:

"We agreed on the following general policies in teaching grammar:

Students in the freshman course should be taught, if they do not already know, certain basic grammatical concepts, so that they may develop their sense of how language works, and thereby how to use it more effectively. They should know enough grammatical terms to carry on analytical and critical discussion of the structure of particular statements."[2]

[1] See Robert C. Pooley, "Problems of Grammar," *Report of the Conference on College Freshman Courses in Composition and Communication* (Chicago, National Council of Teachers of English, 1949), and all issues of *College Composition and Communication* from Vol. I, No. 1 (March, 1950).
[2] *College Composition and Communication*, Vol. I, No. 2 (December, 1950), p. 19.

Other recommendations of this group will be presented below in the discussion of the traditional point of view in grammar.

The workshop group of 1951 presented among their findings the following:

. . . Workshop members agreed that the terminology of grammar is present in Western culture and that it might very well be considered an obligation of the freshman instructor to provide his students with this terminology. It was pointed out in the discussion that in both speaking and writing the student will frequently be confronted with comments like "That is not a very good adjective" or "That adverb was not happily chosen." Some preparation is necessary before the student can interpret such comments.
. . . Workshop members made clear that they would further recommend explaining the terms from a functional standpoint." [3]

Although the agreement concerning the place of grammar in college basic composition is well-nigh universal, the manner in which the grammar is to be taught is less uniform. Among the variations three leading trends can be discerned, which will be treated briefly in succeeding sections of this chapter. By far the largest number of basic composition courses follow what may be called the traditional point of view in the teaching of grammar. This point of view follows the pattern of grammar generally taught in the high schools, it uses the familiar terminology of grammatical elements (though with some variations in specific terms), and it analyzes sentences in the familiar patterns of simple, compound, complex, and compound-complex organizations. The traditional point of view appears in most of the college course outlines, and it is followed with extremely few variations by the publishers of the textbooks and handbooks of composition.

The second trend, comprising a fairly small number of colleges, treats of grammar historically. The emphasis in these courses is not so much upon grammar as a system to be learned and applied as upon grammar as a historical fact, its present condition and terminology being examined as the heritage of a long evolutionary

[3] *Ibid.*, Vol. II, No. 4 (December, 1951), p. 13.

process. This presentation is usually accompanied by some attention to the history of the English language.

The third trend, comprising at present perhaps the smallest number of colleges, but with indications of rapid growth, is the viewing of grammar as the technique of analyzing the structure of English. It discards all grammar of classification and attempts upon objective observation to build a new system of analysis upon a new set of terms, or upon older terms given new precise limitations. In general, this group finds the traditional system of grammar entirely inadequate and offers a new pattern; thus far, however, there has been no general agreement as to what the new pattern should be. These three points of view will be developed and illustrated.

THE TRADITIONAL POINT OF VIEW

Among the traditionalists in the teaching of grammar for college composition may be recognized two schools of thought. One of these might be called "fundamentalist" in defending and practicing a formal presentation of English grammar pretty much as it developed in the nineteenth century, with precise definitions, formal classification of elements, and an uncompromising firmness in logical and grammatical rules as applied to usage. The theory underlying this type of instruction is that a thorough grounding in the entire traditional system of grammar, with unrelaxed attention to traditional patterns of usage, will produce accurate and precise writers in English composition.

The second school of thought might be called "functionalist" because its adherents, while retaining the traditional terms and patterns of analysis, tend to discard matters of formal classification which do not bear upon the analysis of sentence structure, so as to give greater weight and emphasis to those elements which "function" in writing. This group is inclined to be somewhat more lenient in matters of English usage, recognizing the element of change in English usage and permitting those variations of usage which have become reasonably established to be used in written composition, at least in that of an informal nature. To judge from course outlines, the trends in recent manuals of composition, and the discussions at the CCCC meetings, the "functionalist" group is in the majority and is growing in numbers of adherents.

A concise statement of the point of view of the liberal traditionalist may be found in this summary of a workshop group at the CCCC convention of 1950.

We shall teach whatever grammar is necessary to the writing of good informal statements. This means that parts of speech, for example, will be dealt with only as devices to aid the student in understanding relationships within the sentence, and that the emphasis will always be on the relationships, not merely on the definition of and recognition of parts of speech as such. It means that grammar will be used wherever it will contribute to either effectiveness or decency, and never when not related to these aims. [4]

The content of the college composition grammar course may be represented by the following list of matters to teach. It reflects a more or less middle-of-the-road point of view of the traditionalist, not overly formal nor recklessly liberal. It uses the traditional terminology and structure of grammar with an emphasis upon their functional uses.

GRAMMAR ITEMS IN TYPICAL COLLEGE TEXTBOOKS [5]

Parts of speech	*Classification of sentences by form*
noun	simple
verb	compound
pronoun	complex
adjective	compound-complex
adverb	

[4] *Ibid.*, Vol. I, No. 2 (May, 1950), p. 20.

[5] This list was prepared from a comparison of the items included in three currently used texts: Porter G. Perrin, *Writer's Guide and Index to English* (Chicago, Scott, Foresman and Co., 1950); Robert M. Gorrell and Charlton Laird, *Modern English Handbook* (New York, Prentice-Hall, 1953); and John M. Kierzek, *The Macmillan Handbook of English*, 3rd ed. (New York, The Macmillan Co., 1954).

preposition
conjunction
interjection

Verbals
gerund
infinitive
participle

Sentence elements
subject
predicate (verb)
complements
  object
  predicate noun
  predicate adjective
indirect object
phrases
clauses
the concept of subordination

Classification of clauses
adverbial
adjective
noun

Classification of sentences by purpose
declarative
interrogative
imperative
exclamatory

Importance of word order in sentences

Correction of sentence errors

Punctuation of grammatical elements

Grammatical explanations of usage problems

The method of instruction of these materials differs in detail in these three texts as well as in others like them, but certain principles are quite well established. The terms used are defined when they are first presented and are then illustrated in a number of appropriate sentences. These illustrations are discussed, often at some length, to make the use and recognition of the item clear to the student. Then follow exercises, either at this point or at the end of the chapter, to give practice in recognizing and using correctly in sentences the items that have been presented. Review exercises are placed at strategic points, and often a badly mangled passage is presented for the student to improve by the application of the grammatical principles he has learned. Thus it may be seen that in the commonest type of college course, the grammar is presented in traditional terms and with a more or less deductive procedure, but is almost immediately applied to constructive situations to bring out its functional values in the creation and improvement of sentence structure.

The amount of attention to formal analysis of the elements of a sentence varies in the different books. Some are content with the ability to identify and label the chief elements of the sentence; others teach a full system of diagrammatic representation and give exercises in the diagramming of all types of sentences. There is at present no objective evidence to indicate that the use of diagramming more rapidly teaches the elements of grammar or results in the construction of better sentences. On the contrary, all the research evidence available indicates negative results from the teaching of diagramming.

It is very difficult indeed to determine what proportion of time in basic college composition is given to grammar. To judge from some of the textbooks and workbooks, a major share of the total time must go to grammar. On the other hand, there are many teachers who report a major attention to the content of written composition, often reinforced by selected readings, so that in such courses grammar must be much less prominent. One must conclude that in the framework of the traditional presentation of grammar, there is a very wide variety of practice in selection of content, in manner of teaching, and in the allocation of time. While almost everyone agrees that grammar goes with the teaching of composition, there is no agreement as to what amount of grammar or what method of instruction brings about the goal of composition: better writing.

THE HISTORICAL POINT OF VIEW

In a very readable and delightful study of the English language, Laird summarizes his view of English grammar thus:

What are the basic observations to be made about our grammar? . . . For English, surely the following is among the important statements: words placed in patterned relationship combine to complete a predication. For this phenomenon we may best use the word . . . *nexus*, that is, tying together. The second observation is this: English uses subordination. . . . The third observation is this: English uses co-ordination. [6]

[6] Charlton Laird, *The Miracle of Language* (Cleveland, World Publishing Co., 1953).

Viewing English from the perspective of the history of its development, Laird asserts that the basis of the grammar of the English
sentence lies in the terms *nexus, subordination, co-ordination*. He
warns against the idea of "parts of speech" because they are words.
He would have only functions, which he describes thus: being a
subject, being a verb, complementing, modifying, and expressing
relationship. These functions, recognized within the framework of
nexus, subordination, and co-ordination, supply all the analysis
needed to understand the structure of the English sentence.

This brief description may serve to illustrate the method of
approach to grammar of the historical linguist. Generally the linguist is unhappy about the terminology of traditional grammar
because he feels it is inadequate to describe what happens in the use
of English. He combines his skill as a trained observer of language
to analyze the behavior of English today with his scholarship in
the knowledge of the origins and growth of English to create his
own system of analysis which satifies him. So far the historical
linguist has not satisfied any great number of the teachers of
English composition.

In a few institutions, however, a definitely historical approach
to language and grammar in basic composition has been taken.
An excellent illustration may be found in the text prepared for
use at Drake University. [7] In the preface the authors state: "This
book has grown almost entirely out of the thinking and experi-
menting that took place during the development of the present
English program at Drake University. . . . Because all materials
included have been thoroughly tested in terms of objectives, this
resulting text goes far toward providing the content and the practice that are essential in any basic Freshman course." [8] The inherent
point of view in this book is that the student will come to be a
better writer and speaker of his language if he devotes his attention
to the nature of that language, rather than to a formalized termi-

[7] Thomas F. Dunn, Charles A. Ranous, and Harold B. Allen, *Learning Our Language*. Copyright 1950 The Ronald Press Company.
[8] *Ibid.*, p. iii.

nology of it, as in traditional grammar. The book does not repudiate traditional grammar so much as it by-passes it. These are the matters of greater importance:

First, then, the student must learn something of how meaning is conveyed through language, something of the relationship between the word as symbol and the thing for which it stands in a given instance. He must learn what linguists long ago discovered, that meaning is not inherent in the word itself but is determined by the verbal and situational context. . . . Second, besides what the student should learn about language, he must also acquire some elementary knowledge of the laws of thought. . . . Third, the student must learn something of the principles which operate in the selection and ordering of material for linguistic communication. [9]

The authors make clear that factual knowledge of these matters will not of itself make good writers. The student must learn these basic matters in the nature of language, then observe them in the language about him, and finally and constantly practice them in significant communication. Such concentration upon the way language is used will, in the opinion of the authors, go farther in the development of good writers and speakers than does traditional grammar.

THE EXPERIMENTAL POINT OF VIEW

The experimentalists are teachers of basic composition who have been persuaded by recent linguistic research to find the traditional system of English grammar insufficiently precise for the analysis of modern English, and who would substitute a new system for it. Those who write in support of an experimental grammatical system fall into two camps. First are those who feel that the system set up by Fries[10] or that of Whitehall[11] can be

[9] *Ibid.*, pp. iii, iv, v.
[10] Charles C. Fries, *The Structure of English* (New York, Harcourt, Brace and Co., 1952).
[11] Harold Whitehall, *Structural Essentials of English* (New York, Harcourt, Brace and Co., 1956).

applied directly to the basic composition classroom as the means of bringing to the student a technique for the analysis of his language through which his writing can be improved. The second group acknowledge the frontier character of such writers as Fries and Whitehall, but they feel that the suggestions of these linguists are too far removed from practical classroom applications to apply directly, and they call for or outline specific modifications for classroom use. The position of the first group may be found in this statement, though to be fair to the author it must be added that he has elsewhere indicated some need for modification of the findings of primary research for classroom use.

What you think the language is determines how you teach it. Today, an adequate, workable description of English is commonplace in every department of Linguistics in the country. Whenever we take it into the classroom and base our teaching on it, our subject glows with light and interest. We have much to learn about making the best use of it; we have teachers to educate, textbooks to write, practical procedures to work out. A respectable and self-respecting future lies ahead of us, if we resolve to ground our teaching of English on a modern scientific description, in strict and conscientious adherence to the best that is known. Grammar is a ground only, but logic, rhetoric, and stylistics not based on the most adequate grammar known hang on the empty and echoing air. [12]

The crux of this statement lies in the words "an adequate, workable description of English is commonplace...." The supporters of the second position, while acknowledging the pioneer leadership of the linguists, do not find in their work more than a suggestion of the direction to be taken. The road itself has still to be hewed out. The following statement may represent the second point of view:

Mr. Fries says that he hopes his *Structure of English* may serve as a foundation on which practical textbooks may be constructed. I do not think this is possible without a considerable adjustment because I do not think his system will ever be "clearly understood" by anybody but specialists. What we need is a grammatical system which the student

[12] Donald J. Lloyd, "Grammar in Freshman English," *College Composition and Communication,* Vol. V, No. 4 (December, 1954), p. 166.

as well as the professor can understand. To construct such a grammar we must gratefully use the evidence developed by the linguists; but I think we must modify one or two of the conclusions that they have derived from this evidence. [13]

Since a relatively small but very much alive group of composition teachers share the general position as offered by Myers, there can be expected to follow in rapid sequence a number of practical schemes for making effective in the basic composition classroom the structural analysis determined by the linguists. One such scheme may serve as an illustration of the trend. In an article entitled "Let's Teach Grammar Too!" Gates offers a highly simplified structural plan for teaching the elements of the English sentence. [14] He begins, "As a process of language unity, grammar reveals the structural process of writing. The structural process of writing may be expedited by teaching five language blocks—each a basic element of the English sentence. To make the five language blocks function in the student's writing is a primary purpose of teaching the grammatical process." [15] His analysis describes the blocks as follows:

Block one items are labeled S-V-O, the familiar subject-verb-object pattern.

Block two items are word groups which are called 1's: *by the library, on the wall, beyond the atomic era, to run the race, to split the spoils.* It will be seen that 1's are prepositional phrases and infinitive phrases. The author points out that what is important about these phrases is not what they are but what they do, or how they are effectively used.

Block three items are called 2's: *knowing the cause, wanting to be popular, writing on the board, taking defeat.* These will be recognized as participial and gerund phrases. But functionally, Gates points out, it is easy to show that "This language block works with

[13] L. M. Myers, "Linguistics and the Teaching of Rhetoric," *ibid.*, p. 167.
[14] George G. Gates, "Let's Teach Grammar Too!" *College English*, Vol. 17, No. 5 (February, 1956), pp. 306–308.
[15] *Ibid.*, p. 306.

S's and O's (s's and o's, 1's and 3's) but not with V's unless the V is a form of *to be* ..." [16]

Block four items are called 3's: *defeated trying, broken in spirit, sold on the block, caught speeding, known on heaven and earth.* These are past participle phrases; the author points out that they are frequent stumbling blocks to students who, having learned that *defeated* is a verb, can never see it as anything else. Making a workable block of it as a phrasal group helps to remove this difficulty, Gates feels. The student can see graphically that 3's are attached to S's and O's, and cannot stand by themselves. For example, the pattern of the sentence "Prometheus, chained to a rock, endured the agony inflicted upon him by Zeus" is S-V-O. The combinations of S-V-O with 1's, 2's, and 3's provide a simple but accurate pattern of analysis for all simple sentences.

Block five items are labeled s-v-o, the signal of a dependent predication; s-v-o therefore can attach itself to any S, V, O as modifier, or it can replace S or O in any S-V-O pattern. Gates illustrates the use of s-v-o in describing the structure of such a sentence as: "Why a nation invites defeat when its morale provides no strength does not explain why a nation neglects morale when that morale means victory." The pattern comes out thus:

$$(s\text{-}v\text{-}o) \quad V \quad (s\text{-}v\text{-}o)$$
$$s\text{-}v\text{-}o \qquad\qquad s\text{-}v\text{-}o$$

It is too early to state with evidence that such a simplified analysis of the structure of English sentences can replace conventional grammar in the training of college students to write better, but no one can deny the ingenuity of the scheme. Its purpose is clear; to establish a means of studying the patterns of English sentences with a minimum of terminology and a maximum of clarification. Time will tell whether such schemes will take hold and become the means to the teaching of structural grammar. At the moment this trend seems worth watching.

[16] *Ibid.*, p. 307.

THE FUTURE OF GRAMMAR IN COLLEGE COMPOSITION

No one can state with certainty at this time just what direction the teaching of grammar in college composition courses will take. One prediction is reasonably sure: the weight of tradition, habit, early training, and conventional respectability will insure many decades of continued use to the traditional nomenclature and patterns of traditional grammar. It is probable that formal analysis and classification will give way to a more functional approach, but still well within the pattern of standard grammar as it is now known and taught.

On the other hand, the implications of such books as Fries's *The Structure of English* and Whitehall's *Structural Essentials of English* are only just beginning to reach the front line of classroom teachers. As new and simplified schemes of structural analysis become better known, it is reasonable to suppose that many teachers will try them out, and that some, at least, will find them effective. An outstanding textbook adopting a structural plan of grammar analysis could conceivably change the pattern of teaching grammar within a decade in much the same manner as Porter Perrin's *Index to English,* first published in 1939, changed the general attitude toward liberal usage. Perrin's book rode on a growing current of opinion whose foundations had been laid by earlier research workers such as Sterling Andrus Leonard [17] and others. It is very probable that the current research in the analysis of structure in English will develop another current of opinion that in time will bring about a revolution in the theory and practice of English grammar in composition courses. This revolution will have to take place at the college level first, for high school teachers are not apt to adopt systems which are frowned upon by the college teachers to whom they send their graduates. But if the new schemes are adopted generally by colleges, the high schools will be quick to

[17] Sterling Andrus Leonard, *Current English Usage* (Chicago, Inland Press, 1932).

follow. It is not impossible, therefore, that within thirty years a grammar new in terminology and method of instruction may have superseded the pattern inherited from the seventeenth and eighteenth centuries.[18]

REFERENCES

Conference on College Composition and Communication, *College Composition and Communication*, all issues from Vol. I, No. 1 (March, 1950).

DUNN, Thomas F., RANOUS, Charles A., and ALLEN, Harold B., *Learning Our Language* (New York, Ronald Press, 1950).

FRIES, Charles C., *The Structure of English* (New York, Harcourt, Brace and Co., 1952).

LAIRD, Charlton, *The Miracle of Language* (New York, World Publishing Co., 1953).

PERRIN, Porter G., *Index to English* (Chicago, Scott, Foresman and Co., 1939).

ROBERTS, Paul, *Patterns of English* (New York, Harcourt, Brace and Co., 1956).

WHITEHALL, Harold, *Structural Essentials of English* (New York, Harcourt, Brace and Co., 1956).

[18] See Paul Roberts, *Patterns of English,* for the most recent application of structural linguistics to classroom grammar.

XIV

The Evaluation of Grammar Teaching

THE CHIEF PROBLEM in the evaluation of grammar teaching and learning is the uncertainty of the goals or objectives. If grammar is thought of as primarily the source of correctness in speech and writing, the tests of grammar will lay great stress on such matters as the use of *lie* and *lay*, the principal parts of irregular verbs, the case forms of pronouns, and choice among idioms. [1] If grammar is thought of chiefly as a set of definitions and terms to be memorized and identified in the naming of parts of speech and the parts of the sentence, the tests will stress definitions and identification. Finally, if grammar is viewed as the means by which the operational structure of the English sentence can be studied and applied to the process of written communication, as is set forth in this book, then the tests of grammar will endeavor to measure the students' success in understanding structure and applying it effectively to his writing.

The discussion of grammar testing which follows will treat of testing in two divisions: formal, printed, objective-type tests which presumably have standardized norms and can be used for comparative purposes; and informal, classroom, teacher-constructed tests designed for the advancement of instruction as well as its measurement.

[1] Cf. L. J. O'Rourke, *Self-Aids in the Essentials of Grammatical Usage* (Washington, Educational and Personnel Publishing Co., 1927).

STANDARDIZED TESTS

Many of the so-called "English tests" contain exercises in grammar in varying amounts. The kind of grammar presented varies widely from test to test, and is in some cases so confused with usage that none of the English tests described and reviewed in *The Fourth Mental Measurements Yearbook* [2] can be recommended to measure students' knowledge of grammar. Indeed, very few of these tests can be recommended as measurement of success in "English," for their scope is often so narrow, and the English content so limited, that they measure only fragments of the complex art called "English."

The Fourth Mental Measurements Yearbook lists only three tests of specific grammatical knowledge. These are:

1. *Objective Test in Grammar.* Grades 10–12. Published in 1950; Author Nellie F. Falk; Publisher, Perfection Form Co., Logan, Iowa.

2. *Objective Tests in English (Grammar).* Grades 7–9. Published in 1950; Author Gunnar Horn; Publisher, Perfection Form Co., Logan, Iowa.

The first two tests are quite similar in nature and to a large degree in content. Each has an exercise booklet which can be used separately and an answer sheet which constitutes the student's response to the test. What is listed is identification of grammatical elements, recognition of complete and incomplete sentences, and English usage of various kinds. The junior high school test expects knowledge of English sentence structure through compound and complex sentences, including adjective and adverb clauses. But most of the content is devoted to "correctness" in verb use, pronoun use, adjective and adverb use, and so on. The senior high school test includes a larger proportion of space given to grammatical identification, but the majority of exercises deal with correctness, including punctuation. These tests will measure reasonably well how well students have mastered the terminology and

---

[2] Oscar Krisen Buros, *The Fourth Mental Measurements Yearbook* (Highland Park, N.J., The Gryphon Press, 1953), pp. 148–183.

exercises of the standard grammar textbooks, but they cannot and do not measure the ability to use grammar constructively and creatively in the improvement of writing. There are no data regarding the validity and reliability of these tests, and no norms are offered.

3. *Iowa Grammar Information Test.* Grades 7–12. Published in 1935 in two forms, A and B. Authors Fred D. Cram and Harry A. Greene. Publisher, Bureau of Educational Research and Service, State University of Iowa.

Each form of this test consists of 80 exercises of the multiple-response type covering the categories of (*a*) kinds of sentences, (*b*) classes of sentences, (*c*) subject and predicate, (*d*) parts of speech, (*e*) antecedents, (*f*) phrases and clauses, (*g*) complements, (*h*) comparison, (*i*) classification of verbs, (*j*) tense, (*k*) mood, (*l*) person, (*m*) number, (*n*) case, (*o*) gender, (*p*) independent elements. A manual explains the construction of the test forms and presents evidence for the validity and reliability of the test. Norms are provided for grades seven through twelve as of the beginning, middle, and end of the school year.

The authors achieve in this test what they have intended; namely, the measurement of what is retained by students from instruction in formal grammar. No claim is made that the test measures anything else, and the authors commendably refrain from any evaluation of the place of grammar in English communication.

All three of these formal tests are unsatisfactory as a measure of the success of grammar to improve communication. Inasmuch as composition is a combination of a number of highly subjective skills, it seems doubtful that it will ever be measured qualitatively by objective tests. It is unfair to expect these tests to do anything more than to show how well students have learned labels and identifications. But furthermore, these tests suffer from confusions inherent in the teaching of grammar. What clarity of discernment can we expect of a student when the test itself uses such ambiguous definitions as "A sentence that expresses emotion is exclamatory," or "An infinitive phrase is a phrase that begins with *to,* expressed or understood, when the *to* is not used as a preposition"? In the latter case the student is required to identify an infinitive phrase by a *to* that may not be there!

Because standardized tests, at least those now available, will be found unsatisfactory for the measurement of grammatical understanding as it is set forth in this book, the teacher at all levels is advised to make his own tests to measure two basic outcomes of his teaching. These are (1) the student understands the grammatical fact or relationship that has been taught so that he sees it as a part of the language he uses; and (2) he can utilize this fact or relationship himself to build a better, clearer, more interesting sentence than he might have done before. As suggestions for such tests as the teacher will make for his own use, the following samples are offered, illustrating some of the grammatical concepts taught at the various grade levels.

JUNIOR HIGH SCHOOL GRAMMAR TESTS

The purpose of these tests is to give the student an opportunity to demonstrate his grasp of grammatical principles in two practical respects: (1) his recognition of the structural elements of the English sentence by position, use, and name; and (2) to apply the structural elements of the sentence to the creation of his own sentences. The tests presented below are intended as examples of the kinds of tests the teacher will form for himself to measure the extent to which his instruction has given students a workable understanding of grammar.

Group I. Seventh-Grade Tests

A. RECOGNITION OF SUBJECT, VERB, OBJECT

Directions: Write an appropriate word in each blank space. On the line at the right put in the name of the sentence part which you supplied, such as subject, verb, object.

Example: <u>The boys</u> ate some apples.   subject

1. _____ likes milk very much.   _____
2. The principal introduced a distinguished
   _____.   _____
3. Everybody _____ to the circus.   _____
4. Yesterday _____ had an accident.   _____
5. There _____ five books on the shelf.   _____
6. Anybody can throw a _____.   _____
7. _____ took his sister to the movies.   _____
8. The seventh grade _____ a concert.   _____
9. John's mother _____ a fine cake.   _____
10. Tom and Frank _____ a large boat.   _____

B. RECOGNITION OF PARTS OF SPEECH

Directions: Form a sentence from each of the words in the list below. Underline the word in your sentence, and in the margin at the right show what part of speech it is in your sentence by writing noun, pronoun, adjective, adverb, or verb.

Example: John <u>drove</u> the family car.   verb

a. Alice	*f.* school	_____
b. ran	*g.* broke	_____
c. they	*h.* happily	_____
d. soon	*i.* we	_____
e. fast	*j.* strong	_____

C. RECOGNIZING SENTENCE COMPLETENESS

Directions: In each of the following groups of words some necessary part of the sentence is missing. Examine each group, and in the space at the right, name the part of the sentence that is needed.

Examples: *a.* likes to walk in the country   subject

b. The careless boys broke . . .   object

c. No one at the store . . .   verb

d. The last class was . . .   complement

1. Everyone to the picnic at the grove _____
2. All the packages were very _____
3. Brought his mother to school _____
4. The clever boys had made _____
5. Near the edge the ice seems _____
6. At evening the sun below the western clouds _____
7. A most startling aroused the neighborhood _____
8. Frank, this is _____
9. The heavy car across the road and into the ditch _____
10. Had been taken to the circus by his uncle _____

D. USING ADJECTIVES AND NOUNS TO COMPLETE SENTENCES

Directions: Certain verbs like *is, was, were, seems,* etc., do not take an object but are followed by a noun or adjective to complete the thought. An adjective used this way is called a predicate adjective (P.A.) and a noun used this way is called a predicate noun (P.N.). Complete the following sentences by using words from the list below. In the space at the right, place P.A. where you use an adjective, and P.N. where you use a noun.

   List of words: friend, red, useful, captain, rough, beautiful, taller, safe, steep, city

1. The old barn had been painted _____ _____
2. The girls chose Pat to be the _____ _____
3. The spring flowers were especially _____ _____
4. No one thinks the ice is _____ yet _____
5. The mountains here are very _____ _____
6. Everyone says New York is a fine _____ _____
7. John is _____ than Frank _____
8. After the storm the waves will be _____ _____
9. The old mill seemed to be no longer _____ _____
10. Frances is my best _____ _____

E. DISTINGUISHING PREDICATE ADJECTIVES AND NOUNS FROM DIRECT OBJECTS

Directions: Each of the following sentences needs a single word to complete it. Supply a word for each sentence, and in the space at the right indicate whether you have supplied a direct object (D.O.), a predicate noun (P.N.), or a predicate adjective (P.A.).

Examples: All nations desire peace	D.O.
Some wild animals seem friendly	P.A.
The guilty person was Tom	P.N.

1. Everybody says the weather will be _____   _____
2. The boy chosen to lead was _____   _____
3. The skidding car broke down a _____   _____
4. The team elected a new _____   _____
5. How did you catch so large a _____?   _____
6. Did the meeting seem too _____?   _____
7. The boss gave Tom a _____   _____
8. These problems look _____   _____
9. Mother, this is _____   _____
10. At the end of the day the grocer
    closed his _____   _____

F. CONSTRUCTIVE KNOWLEDGE OF THE SIMPLE SENTENCE

Directions: The names of some sentence patterns are given below. In the space below each pattern write a sentence which is constructed according to the pattern. Use *the, a, an* and modifiers where needed.

Example: subject-verb-object
         The hungry boys ate all the ice cream.

1. subject-verb-object
2. subject-verb-predicate adjective
3. Question: verb-subject-verb-object.
4. Command: verb-object
5. subject-verb-predicate noun
6. subject-verb
7. Question: verb-subject-predicate noun
8. subject-verb-object
9. subject-verb
10. subject-verb-predicate noun.

Group II. Tests to Add for Eighth Grade

A. MAKING COMPOUND SENTENCES

Directions: Show how you would form a compound sentence from two simple sentences by writing an appropriate conjunction (*and, but, yet, or, for*) in the space at the right of each pair of sentences.

1. The boys went to the church supper. . . .
   Their parents went also.   _____

2. No special plans were made for the party. . . .
   Everyone had a good time.   _____

3. Jack led the team on to the field. . . . He had
   been elected captain.   _____

4. Bring your electric lantern with you. . . . Else
   we shall have to use candles.   _____

5. The police expected trouble at the rally. . . .
   Everyone behaved very well.   _____

B. USING CONJUNCTIONS IN COMPOUND SENTENCES

Directions: For each of the following conjunctions write a compound sentence using the conjunction so as to bring out its meaning clearly.

Example: Jane thought her dress was too long, <u>yet</u> all her friends admired it.

Use these conjunctions: *and, for, but, yet, or.*

C. MAKING COMPOUND PARTS OF SENTENCES

Directions: One part of each of the following sentences is underlined. Over the underlined part write a parallel, compound part, introduced by a conjunction.

and his science.

Examples: a. Bob studied <u>his history</u>

and tugged

       b. The children <u>pulled</u> the wagon over the rough ground.

1. The <u>horses</u> were gathered in the barn.
2. <u>No snow</u> was predicted for tomorrow.

3. The engineers examined the new car thoroughly.
4. Mary helped by washing the dishes.
5. The new flag-pole was tall.
6. Harry took the ski club to a new hill.
7. To go to New York, Henry went to the railway station.
8. For the party mother spent most of the day making sand-wiches.

D. USING PREPOSITIONAL PHRASES AS MODIFIERS

Directions: Rewrite each of the following sentences, adding a prepo-sitional phrase according to the suggestion in parentheses.

1. The leader gave directions.   (leader of what?)
2. At the end stood a tumble-down building.   (end of what?)
3. Five flocks flew rapidly westward.   (flocks of what?)
4. The poorly constructed tower fell.   (where?)
5. The debating team came.   (by what means?)
6. In autumn the migrating birds fly.   (where?)
7. The car skidded wildly.   (where?)
8. Kind neighbors brought the tired child home.   (when?)
9. The Saxons fought bravely.   (for what?)
10. Ted got six tickets.   (from whom?)

E. USING INDIRECT OBJECTS

Directions: Rewrite each of the following sentences inserting an indirect object at the proper place. Underline the indirect object.

Example: Mother gave some ice cream to the children.
Mother gave the children some ice cream.

1. The child brought an apple for the teacher.
2. No one gave any thought to me.
3. The class took some flowers to the sick child.
4. The gardener gave some water to the plants.
5. Nobody thought to give tickets to them.

F. DISTINGUISHING DIRECT AND INDIRECT OBJECTS

Directions: In the following sentences write the letters DO over each direct object, and IO over each indirect object. Some sentences will lack one or both.

1. The active child gave his toys a hard life.
2. Father brought a basket of apples from the farm.
3. Give me that watch!
4. Take all your books back to school.
5. My uncles brought us drawing materials.
6. No one gave the floor a good scrubbing.
7. Frank spent all his money for a radio.
8. John gave the old porter a generous tip.
9. No one believed him any more.
10. This test will give you some practice.

Group III. Tests to Add for Ninth Grade

Any or all of the preceding tests are valid for review of the simple sentence and its functional parts. After adequate instruction and practice the following tests may be used, particularly at the end of the ninth year as evaluation of learning in the new concepts.

A. USING PARTICIPIAL PHRASES

Directions: Rewrite each of the following sentences utilizing the statement in parentheses as a participial phrase.

Example: The boy went home. (He had finished his work)
Having finished his work, the boy went home.

1. I discovered that *Robinson Crusoe* was missing. (I was looking over my books.)
2. The beavers built a substantial dam. (They cut down aspen trees alongside the pond.)
3. Mary went to the movies. (She had studied and washed the dinner dishes.)
4. The workmen had difficulty in moving the lumber. (The

lumber had swollen because of the rain.) (Note: be careful on this one and the next!)

5. The old car wheezed and chugged its way up the mountain. (We had eaten our lunch.)

B. CHANGING STATEMENTS TO SUBORDINATE ADVERBIAL CLAUSES

Directions: In the margin at the right, place a connecting adverb (*where, when, as, since, because,* etc.) which will make the first statement of each pair below dependent upon the second. Correct the punctuation between the statements and change capital letters where necessary.

1. We arrived at the station. The train from Chicago had already come in. _____

2. The child had sticky marks around her mouth. I knew she had eaten the candy. _____

3. The last war came to an end. Military training has been required of all young men. _____

4. I was getting supper ready. Nearly all of the guests arrived. _____

5. You take in the plates. Please wash your hands carefully. _____

C. WRITING COMPLEX SENTENCES WITH ADVERBIAL CLAUSES

Directions: To each of the following statements add your own adverbial clause according to the suggestion in parentheses.

1. The hot-dish came out of the oven. (when?)
2. The small boy was crying. (why?)
3. No one thought of going home. (when?)
4. Many people take out insurance too late. (when?)
5. The dentist continued to talk. (during what time?)

D. DISTINGUISHING SIMPLE AND COMPLEX SENTENCES

Directions: After each simple sentence below write S; after each complex sentence write C.

1. John brought his roommate home for the holidays and introduced him to his parents. _____

2. While all the snowplows cleared the roads, the stalled cars lined up for miles.   _____

3. The crowd went home after the excitement had died down.   _____

4. To win the race and get the athletic letter was the leading ambition of every track man.   _____

5. Before you go home, please finish these letters.   _____

SENIOR HIGH SCHOOL GRAMMAR TESTS

For review purposes and for practice in the formation of simple sentences and complex sentences of the adverbial modifier type, the preceding exercises for grades seven through nine may be used for teaching and evaluation. For example, a practical diagnostic test for the opening of the tenth year can be formed by selecting and assembling exercises from a number of the preceding tests, or by writing similar exercises, to ascertain the command of sentence structure held by members of an incoming tenth-grade class. Those exercises easily performed by the group will need no review, whereas those which cause difficulty for any number of students may be taken as the first elements of instruction in the tenth-grade grammar program. For those concepts of grammar which appear for the first time in the tenth grade and beyond, the following exercises may serve as tests of success in learning.

Group IV. Tests for the Tenth Year

A. USING ADJECTIVE CLAUSES

Directions: Combine the following groups of sentences using *who, whom, that, which,* and *whose* as relative pronouns to introduce adjective clauses.

1. My mother entertained an old friend, Mrs. Hanson. Mrs. Hanson has traveled extensively.

2. I told you to use those books. The books came from the library.
3. Alice is my friend. I am very fond of her.
4. This is the car. I told you about it. Its design was announced in the papers.
5. Roses were given away free. Everyone got one.

B. CREATE YOUR OWN ADJECTIVE CLAUSE SENTENCES BY EMPLOYING THE FOLLOWING RELATIVE PRONOUNS AS INDICATED

Example: who—The boy who came late is my brother.

1. who	5. whose
2. that	6. from which
3. which	7. of whom
4. to whom	8. for whom

C. RECOGNIZING RESTRICTIVE AND NONRESTRICTIVE CLAUSES

Directions: Each adjective clause below which clearly limits or describes or identifies the noun that it modifies is a *restrictive clause.* Restrictive clauses use no punctuation. Each adjective clause which adds information to an antecedent already defined is called a *nonrestrictive clause.* Nonrestrictive clauses are set off in commas. The only reason for distinguishing one from another is to punctuate the sentence correctly. Place commas before and after each *nonrestrictive* clause.

Examples: The man *who just entered* is my uncle.
The summit of Mount Ranier, *which is often obscured by clouds,* is 14,408 feet above sea level.

1. The things that I want to do will take a lot of time.
2. The Twentieth Century Limited which regularly runs to Chicago was halted at Cleveland by snow.
3. My fussy old aunt who dislikes children was surprisingly patient with Timmy.
4. All products which are attractively packaged tend to sell better than others.
5. Old Colonel Humphries whose friends actively supported his nomination made a glorious campaign for election as sheriff.

D. USING CLAUSES AS NOUNS

Directions: Combine the pairs of ideas below into sentences in which one statement becomes the subject or object of the verb in the other statement.

> *Examples:* No one opposed Henry's election to the club. This fact surprised Henry.
>
> That no one opposed Henry's election to the club surprised him.

1. No one did any homework. The teacher discovered this.
2. The world is flat. This was believed for many centuries.
3. All of us should have a vacation. Mother urged this.
4. Where he should go next. This puzzled Henry.
5. Hard physical work strengthens the body. This fact was discovered by the young recruits.

E. USING APPOSITION EFFECTIVELY TO SUBORDINATE AN IDEA

Directions: Rewrite the following groups of words into one sentence in which one idea is subordinated to another idea by being placed *in apposition* to it.

> *Example:* Tom brought home his shop project. It was a well-made table lamp.
>
> Tom brought home his shop project, *a well-made table lamp.*

1. The girls' contribution to the picnic was a great success. They brought an iced layer cake.
2. The new pavement on Highway 30 has improved the ease of riding. Poured concrete was used.
3. Jane's boat sailed better after she had added ballast. Jane sails a sloop.
4. John proudly introduced his new friend. This friend is a student from Germany.
5. At the end of the tournament dad brought home his prize. It was a large silver loving cup.

Group V. Tests for the Eleventh Year

These tests provide a measuring device for the new grammatical elements introduced in the eleventh year. Naturally all the sentence structure previously taught will need to be reviewed and practiced from time to time, both by the use of exercises such as appear in this chapter, and by the writing of paragraphs by students which are then analyzed for structure as in the example on page 197.

A. USING GERUND PHRASES AND INFINITIVE PHRASES AS VARIOUS
   PARTS OF THE SENTENCE STRUCTURE

Directions: A gerund phrase may be a subject of a verb, the object of a verb, or the object of a preposition. Examples of gerund phrases: *making boats, preparing dinner, chopping wood*, etc. Create your own sentences making use of gerund phrases as indicated.

1. Gerund phrase as subject of the sentence.
2. Gerund phrase as object of a verb.
3. Gerund phrase as predicate noun.
4. Gerund phrase object of the preposition *from*.
5. Gerund phrase following the pronoun *his*.
6. Gerund phrase following the pronoun *their*.

Infinitive phrases are used as subjects of verbs, objects of verbs, and as adjective and adverb modifiers.

Examples of infinitive phrases: *to cut the grass, to believe his story, to calculate the risk*, etc. Create your own sentences using infinitive phrases as indicated.

1. Infinitive phrase as subject of a verb.
2. Infinitive phrase as object of a verb.
3. Infinitive phrase as predicate noun.
4. Infinitive phrase modifying a noun.
5. Infinitive phrase modifying a verb.
6. Infinitive phrase in apposition to a noun.

B. USING MODIFYING ELEMENTS EFFECTIVELY

Directions: Many sentences are rendered unclear or awkward by the improper placement of a modifying word, phrase, or clause. In each of the following sentences draw a line under any modifying element which you feel is misplaced, and by a caret (∧) indicate where it should be inserted.

    Example: The work ∧ took a long time *that I had to do.*

1. The friend failed me in an emergency that I counted on.
2. The salesman put the lamp in the show window which was to be sold.
3. The boys brought mother a gift and placed it on the table for Mother's Day.
4. Many books are hard to read by foreign authors.
5. The water-color sketches were hung along the walls of scenes from the seaside.
6. The shirts got lost in the mail that you sent back to me.

Group VI. Tests for the Twelfth Year

The emphasis in the twelfth year should be upon the utilization of grammatical knowledge in the writing of accurate, varied, and pleasing English sentences. Toward this goal two types of exercises are suggested. Exercise A measures ability to identify and use creatively the various patterns of the English sentence. Exercise B leads the student to analyze his own writing to ascertain what variety of structures he is employing.

A. BUILDING SENTENCES TO ORDER

Directions: Apply your knowledge of sentence structure by creating a meaningful English sentence for each of the patterns indicated below.

1. Begin with "there," and let the subject follow the verb.
2. Begin with a participial phrase.
3. Make a complex sentence which begins with an adverbial modifier.
4. Write a sentence in which the subject is modified by a non-restrictive adjective clause.
5. Use an infinitive as subject of the sentence.
6. Use a gerund phrase as object of a preposition.

7. Write a compound sentence joined by "yet."
8. Write a complex sentence whose subject is a noun clause.
9. Write a compound-complex sentence in which the second independent clause is modified by an adverbial clause.
10. Write a sentence containing three parallel objects of a single verb.

B. ANALYZING THE SENTENCE STRUCTURE OF A PARAGRAPH

Directions: Read carefully the sentences of the paragraph below and note how they are analyzed by number. When you are sure you understand the method of analysis, select a paragraph of at least six sentences from one of your own compositions and analyze the structure in the same way.

READING ESSAYS

1. The essay is designed to be read rather than studied. 2. That is, the author assumes that you will sit relaxed in a comfortable chair with a good light to lend him your attention as you follow his train of thought, whether it is humorous, whimsical, or serious. 3. Consequently this book has been planned with the idea that the essays themselves are of first importance; the notes and biographies have been added to enhance the enjoyment of each essay by telling you something about its author, explaining difficult words and allusions, offering questions to ask yourself after reading, and listing other writings by the same author you might enjoy finding to read. 4. But the important thing is to read, enjoy, and understand the essays themselves.

ANALYSIS OF SENTENCES ABOVE

Type of sentence	Kind of beginning	Special features
1. Simple	Subject first	Parallel infinitives
2. Complex	Introductory clause	Noun clause object of verb
3. Compound-complex	Adverb	Parallel gerund phrases
4. Simple	Conjunction	Parallel infinitives

COLLEGE FRESHMAN GRAMMAR TEST

This is the type that might be used diagnostically at the beginning of the college freshman year, as an inventory of student ability to use effectively grammatical knowledge in sentence building. The emphasis is therefore upon active use of grammar rather than upon definition and identification. The same test, or one made parallel to it, might be used at the end of a semester or a year to note the progress of the student in his application of grammar to composition.

A Sample College Level Test of Grammatical Knowledge

I. BASIC SENTENCE STRUCTURE

Directions: Some of the following word groups are complete sentences. Others require one of the following grammatical elements for their completion: subject, verb, object, predicate complement, independent clause. After each group which is complete, write the word *complete*. After each group which is incomplete, write the name of the grammatical element needed for completion.

1. The sun rose splendidly in a sky speckled with light, fleecy clouds . . . _____
2. No wind in spite of the appearance of clouds associated with the movement of air . . . _____
3. Which puzzled all the observers . . . _____
4. The coloring of the sky, soft and gentle, seemed . . . _____
5. Had gathered all the loose articles from the clothes line before the storm could strike . . . _____
6. Beginning with a few large drops, the rain gradually increased in volume to a full downpour . . . _____
7. Having soaked the earth for three hours and filled the streams and rivers to their banks . . . _____

8. The children gathered long sticks to build . . .   _____

9. When the storm was finally ended and the heavy clouds moved away . . .   _____

10. To get the most good from the storm and to utilize the excess water to the best advantage . . .   _____

II. VARIETY OF SENTENCE STRUCTURE

Note carefully the ideas presented by this sentence. *Many angry motorists the next day demanded an immediate repeal of the unpopular law.*

Directions: Rewrite this sentence according to the instructions given after each number. All necessary changes may be made, but no new ideas must be added, nor any essential idea omitted.

1. Begin with the adverb phrase of time.
2. Begin with the complete object of the verb *demanded*.
3. Begin with *This unpopular law*.
4. Using the verb *came* rewrite the sentence to include a participial phrase.

III. SELECTION OF APPROPRIATE SENTENCE STRUCTURES

Directions: Place a circle around the letter of the sentence in each group below which has the most effective structure for its purpose.

1. (*a*) The definition of clamming is the art or science of extricating the clam from its native mud.
   (*b*) Clamming may be defined as the art or science of extricating the clam from his native mud.
   (*c*) Getting the clam out of his native mud, this may be defined as clamming.

2. (*a*) Such was his fame, that if his sword but clacked a warning on the pavement, it must have brought the apprentices to the windows.
   (*b*) When his sword clacked a warning on the pavement, he

was so famous that it had to bring the apprentices to the windows.

(*c*) Getting the clam out of his native mud, this may be sword of this famous man make a clack on the pavements.

3. (*a*) You are too proud to feel that your decision, though sudden, is irrevocable, because you don't want to go back.

(*b*) You feel that your decision, because going back would mean death to your pride, is irrevocable, though sudden.

(*c*) You feel that your decision, though sudden, is irrevocable, because going back would mean death to your pride.

4. (*a*) You will perceive, if not at once, later, that you have bitten off just about as much as you can chew.

(*b*) You will later perceive that you have bitten off just about as much as you can chew, if not at once.

(*c*) If not at once you will perceive later that you have bitten off just about as much as you can chew.

5. (*a*) The pup-dog is the best of companions in the open, his exuberant vitality and unquenchable zest for things give him endless variety in general.

(*b*) The pup-dog in the open is the best of companions; his exuberant vitality and unquenchable zest for things in general give him endless variety.

(*c*) The best of companions in the open is the exuberant vitality and unquenchable zest of the pup-dog for things in general that give him endless variety.

IV. SUBORDINATION

Directions: Groups of ideas are given below in short sentences or fragments. In each case combine the group of ideas into one sentence, using the grammatical devices of subordination as indicated.

1. It was a fine day. Father proposed a drive in the car.
   Convert the first idea into an adverbial clause of reason.

2. My mother has a childhood friend. Her name is Ann Harris. She came to visit us.

Make one subject-verb group of these ideas, in which *Ann Harris* stands in apposition to *friend*.

3. The school census was taken. This task occupied four days of the ladies' time.

Convert the first idea into a gerund phrase which is subject of the verb *occupied*.

4. Allen had a cup of coffee. He was going to New York. This was before the plane left.

Make one sentence beginning with an adverbial clause of time.

5. During the months of July and August. Cabins may be rented for reasonable prices. They are located by the sea shore.

Make one sentence in which the third statement is reduced to a prepositional phrase in its proper place.

V. IMPROVING AWKWARD CONSTRUCTIONS

Directions: Some of the following sentences are unclear because of the misplacement of modifiers. Others lack parallel structure. Still others lack grammatical agreement. In each case revise or rewrite the sentence to secure the highest degree of grammatical propriety and clarity of meaning.

1. The only section of Europe I have visited frequently are the British Isles.
2. I have never owned a motor boat and do not consider it for the future.
3. As a child I grew up in a large city, and now that I live in the country I find that it is a handicap.
4. Taking a quick look at the clock, the train was due to arrive at any moment.
5. When only a child my father took the whole family to visit Washington, D.C.
6. My legs failed me after hearing the news.
7. Arriving at the campsite the boys cut wood, built a large fire, and their supper was quickly prepared.
8. While traveling in the Mediterranean a lame foot prevented my climbing Mount Olympus.

9. First choose your courses, then fill out all the cards, and finally fees must be paid.

10. Coming at last to the top of the high hill, the glorious skyline of New York was clearly seen.

11. A list of all the courses I had taken with the grades were sent to the college registrar.

12. We should avoid entanglements with aggressive nations, and even with those contemplating it.

13. I cannot either object or agree with your ideas.

14. One should begin early in the morning, for you are at your best then, and the task is quickly done.

15. In spite of delays, those who are injured in the end are carefully treated.

16. If the water in the fish bowl should become stale, it must be changed and put in fresh.

17. There is a record of all students who were caught smoking in the Dean's files.

18. Tom's grades were still unsatisfactory to graduate.

19. To save ourselves trouble, many inventions have relieved the task of housekeeping.

20. Bill copied his report out of the *Encyclopaedia Britannica*, which was stupid.

Additional
Reading

The books most directly related to the chapters of this volume are listed at the end of each chapter. For the student desiring to explore the subject of grammar beyond the scope of this book the following readings are suggested.

THE BACKGROUND OF ENGLISH GRAMMAR

BRYANT, Margaret M., *A Functional English Grammar* (Boston, D. C. Heath and Co., 1945).

CURME, George O., *Syntax* (Boston, D. C. Heath and Co., 1931).

JESPERSEN, Otto, *Essentials of English Grammar* (New York, Henry Holt and Co., 1933).

KRAPP, George P., *The Knowledge of English* (New York, Henry Holt and Co., 1927).

MYERS, L. M., *American English, A Twentieth-Century Grammar* (Englewood Cliffs, N. J., Prentice-Hall, Inc., 1952).

ROBERTS, Paul, *Understanding Grammar* (New York, Harper and Bros., 1954).

GRAMMAR AND USAGE

FRIES, Charles C., *American English Grammar*, English Monograph No. 10 of the National Council of Teachers of English (New York, Appleton-Century-Crofts, Inc., 1941).

HALL, Robert A., Jr., *Leave Your Language Alone!* (Ithaca, N. Y., Linguistica, 1950).

KENNEDY, Arthur G., *English Usage*, English Monograph No. 15 of the National Council of Teachers of English (New York, Appleton-Century-Crofts, Inc., 1942).

LEONARD, Sterling A., *The Doctrine of Correctness in English Usage, 1700–1800*, University of Wisconsin Studies in Language and Literature, No. 25 (Madison, Wis., 1929).

MARCKWARDT, Albert H., and WALCOTT, Fred G., *Facts About Current English Usage*, English Monograph No. 7 of the National Council of Teachers of English (New York, Appleton-Century-Crofts, Inc., 1938).

GRAMMAR IN AMERICAN EDUCATION

BRYANT, Margaret M., and AIKEN, Janet R., *Psychology of English* (New York, Columbia University Press, 1940).

DEBOER, John J., KAULFERS, Walter V., and MILLER, Helen R., *Teaching English in Secondary Schools* (New York, McGraw-Hill Book Co., Inc., 1951).

FRIES, Charles C., *Teaching of English* (Ann Arbor, George Wahr, 1948.

HOOK, Julius N., *The Teaching of High School English* (New York, The Ronald Press Co., 1950).

Kansas State Department of Education, *Suggested Standards in Composition for High School English*, Bulletin of the Kansas State Department of Education and the Kansas Education Association, 1948.

MIRRIELEES, Lucia B., *Teaching Composition and Literature in High School*, rev. ed. (New York, Harcourt, Brace and Co., Inc., 1951).

POLLOCK, Thomas Clark, and Others, for the Modern Language Association of America, *The English Language in American Education* (New York, Modern Language Association of America, 1945).

Progressive Education Association, Commission on the Secondary Curriculum, *Language in General Education* (New York, Appleton-Century-Crofts, Inc., 1940).

STRICKLAND, Ruth G., *The Language Arts in the Elementary School* (Boston, D. C. Heath and Co., 1951).

Index

205